SALT TO HONEY

RECIPES FOR GREAT GATHERINGS

Junior League of Salt Lake City, Inc.

PRESENTING SPONSOR

GEORGE S. AND DOLORES DORÉ ECCLES
FOUNDATION

Building on a 20-year tradition of support for the
Junior League of Salt Lake City,
the George S. and Dolores Doré Eccles Foundation
is proud to assist in funding this cookbook,
celebrating the League's 80th Anniversary
of service to our community,
and furthering its ability to enrich the lives of women and children
in Salt Lake City for years to come.

IN TRIBUTE TO

Dolores Doré "Lolie" Eccles

1902–1994
Founding Member, Junior League of Ogden, Utah
Sustaining Member, Junior League of Salt Lake City, Utah

GEORGE S. AND DOLORES DORÉ ECCLES FOUNDATION DIRECTORS

Spencer F. Eccles • Lisa Eccles • Robert M. Graham

SALT TO HONEY

RECIPES FOR GREAT GATHERINGS

Junior League of Salt Lake City, Inc.

SALT TO HONEY

RECIPES FOR GREAT GATHERINGS

Copyright © 2012 by
Junior League of Salt Lake City, Inc.
526 East 300 South
Salt Lake City, Utah 84102
801-328-1019

Photography © by Paula Jansen

Published by

Favorite Recipes® Press

An imprint of

SOUTHWESTERN
Publishing Group, Inc.

P.O. Box 305142
Nashville, Tennessee 37230
1-800-358-0560

Art Director and Book Design: Steve Newman
Project Editor: Tanis Westbrook

Library of Congress Control Number: 2011935833
ISBN: 978-0-9616972-3-5

Manufactured in the United States of America
First Printing: 2012
15,000 copies

**JUNIOR LEAGUE OF
SALT LAKE CITY**

Women building better communities®

Junior League of Salt Lake City
526 East 300 South
Salt Lake City, Utah 84102
801-328-1019

For additional copies of
Salt to Honey: Recipes for Great Gatherings,
please visit our website www.jlslc.org
or call the Junior League of Salt Lake City.

Denotes vintage recipes from
our previous cookbooks,
Heritage, A Pinch of Salt Lake,
and *Always in Season.*

DEDICATION

————

To our community who generously donated more than
a thousand recipes toward this cookbook;

To those who tested and tasted recipes, sometimes with trepidation,
only to discover a new favorite food or preparation;

To those who gathered their friends and families for countless tastings
and their unabashed feedback and suggestions;

To our ever-supportive community partners and their
vision for what the world can become;

To all of those who love food and love sharing it, because memories are
borne of sharing the best of what we have with those we know and those we hope to;

To the people, places and gatherings in our lives,
WE LOVINGLY DEDICATE THIS BOOK.

SALT TO HONEY
RECIPES FOR GREAT GATHERINGS

Committee

Heidi Makowski, *Committee Director* • Daralyn Christensen, *Recipe Chair*
Penny Jensen Sandberg, *Marketing Chair* • Polly Unruh, *Design Chair* • Jessica Weber, *Technology Chair*
Sarah Atzet • Haley Baronne • Kelley Beaudry • Sara Becker • Cara Jones
Tawni Christopherson Russo • Angela Sampinos • Jamie Treend • Sarah Waters • Elizabeth Weeks

Professional Services

Kimberly Astin, *Writer* • Lisa Graham, *External Marketing Director*
Paula Jansen, *Photographer* • Susan Massey, *Food Stylist*

Cover

Salt courtesy of Redmond Incorporated • Honey courtesy of Miller's Honey Company

JUNIOR LEAGUE OF SALT LAKE CITY, INC.

**JUNIOR LEAGUE OF
SALT LAKE CITY**
Women building better communities®

The Junior League of Salt Lake City is a charitable organization of women committed to promoting voluntarism, developing the potential of women and improving communities through the effective action, education, and leadership of trained volunteers.

—Mission Statement

The Junior League of Salt Lake City is proud to publish our fourth cookbook during our 80th anniversary as one of the premiere volunteer organizations in Salt Lake City. In the past eight decades our projects and programs have served our community in the areas of medical, health, cultural, social, and educational needs.

PROJECTS PAST, PRESENT, AND ONGOING

1930s
Children's Service Society
Children's Theater Project
Family Service Society
Junior Programs in the Arts/
    Strawbridge Ballet
Neighborhood House Baby Clinics and
    Nursery Schools
YWCA

1940s
Art Barn
Camp Kearns
Central Volunteer Bureau
Cerebral Palsy Clinic for State of Utah
Community Arts Council
Girl Scouts/Helen Means Camper Fund
Juvenile Court
Traveler's Aid Society
"Up and Down the Scales" Radio
Utah Board of Education and Salt Lake
    Public Library
Utah Red Cross
Visiting Nurse Association

1950s
Community Information Center
Fairmont School for Mentally
    Challenged Children
Hearing and Speech Foundation
Mental Health Association
"Number Seven Sunny Street"—KUED
Recreational Therapy for Children with
    Disabilities
Salt Lake Board of Education

1960s
Community Mental Health Center
Community Training for
    Mentally Challenged Adults
Hogle Zoo
Holladay Children Center's Group Home
Juvenile Court
Salt Lake Art Center
Salt Lake School District—
    School Volunteer Pilot Program
Utah Heritage Foundation
Utah Museum of Natural History

Projects Past, Present, and Ongoing

1970s
Art Start in Salt Lake, Granite, Davis, Murray, and Jordan School Districts
Family Support Center
Junior Achievement
Junior Science Academy at the Utah Museum of Natural History
Juvenile Court
KUER
PACT (Parents and Children Together)
Pine Canyon Boys Ranch
Rape Recovery Center
Repertory Dance Theater
Salt Lake City Court Resource Center
Utah Opera
Wheeler Farm

1980s
Child Care Connection
55+ Senior Citizens Service Directory
Ronald McDonald House
Salt Lake Community Shelter
"Star" at Hansen Planetarium
You're In Charge

1990s
Arts of the Challenged
Alliance House
CARE (Community Assistance Resource Event) Fair
Children's Justice Center
Encore Breast Cancer Survivor Support Program
Environmental Education Summit
Here to Help Pregnancy Prevention Program
Kidspace—Salt Lake Art Center
Omnibus: Gifted and Talented Education Program
Utah AIDS Foundation
Share Your Heart and Home
The Sharing Place
Women Helping Women
Y Teen Home

2000s
Celebration of Life
Kids in the Kitchen
RISE (Refugee Integration into Society through Education)

2010s
EPIC (Educating Parents/ Investing in Children)

Since 1931, the Junior League of Salt Lake City has been building leaders within our community. The Junior League of Salt Lake City provides time, money, volunteers, and leadership for our community. We are unique among other service organizations in that we always pair the money we raise for projects with trained volunteers. Through services to and collaborations with our community, we contribute more than $220,000 and 23,000 volunteer hours annually. Our members are career women, working mothers, stay-at-home moms, and full- and part-time volunteers. We represent a variety of races, religions, and ethnic origins, but we are brought together by a common vision to identify the needs and create positive change for all women, children, and families through collaborative programs and effective advocacy by providing time, money, volunteers, and leadership for our community. We are a legacy of women making a difference.

WELCOME

—————

Fresh—Local—Appetizing—Approachable: this is the inspiration for the recipes we have waiting for you. These flavorful recipes have been shared, tested, tasted, and carefully selected by members of our community. Their generosity and spirit are infused in every page of this book. These recipes are sure to be among your favorites and enjoyed at gatherings of every type for years to come.

One of our goals with this book was to recognize and give back to the community beyond our Junior League volunteer efforts. Therefore, we've included local farmers and food artisans, along with our friends and families, in this project. By supporting local businesses, we lessen the impact on our environment and build the health of our community. Strengthening these connections in our society creates gifts that multiply as they are shared with one another.

Food and togetherness go hand-in-hand. Whether it is a weekly club meeting, a special occasion, breakfast for your family, or dinner for two, these meals all focus on coming together, connecting, and sharing. Thus, our vision for this book: to complete the circle of gathering, giving, and enjoying life. Dig in!

CONTENTS

———

BEGINNINGS

10

SIPS & SNACKS

36

SMALL PLATES

70

LARGE PLATES

116

ON THE SIDE

170

ENDINGS

194

Contributors

227

Index

231

BEGINNINGS

Bacon, Leek and Cheddar Cheese Mini Quiches 12 • Lobster Quiche 13

Vegetable Quiche 13 • Jalapeño Goat Cheese Frittata 15

Shirred Pancetta and Arugula Eggs 16 • Egg Casserole 16 • Sunday Eggs 17

Potato, Eggs and Chorizo Tacos 18 • Chile Relleno Casserole 19

Zucchini Sausage Squares 19 • Salmon and Grits 20 • French Toast with Pecans 21

Raspberry Pancakes 23 • Banana Pancakes 24 • Buttermilk Syrup 24

Perfect Waffles 25 • Waffles Deluxe 25 • Peach Scones 26

Walnut Shortcake Biscuits 26 • Almond Biscotti 27 • Chocolate Zucchini Bread 27

Hazelnut Zucchini Bread 28 • Chunky Monkey Cinnamon Bread 29

Apple Pecan Streusel Muffins 30 • Blueberry Crumble Muffins 31

Nutty Honey Granola 33 • Greek Yogurt, Honey and Poppy Seeds with Blackberries 33

Fresh Fruit with Orange Cream 34 • Fresh Fruit Salad 34

Lime Rum Marinated Fruit 35 • Miller's Basic Honey Butter with Variations 35

Bacon, Leek and Cheddar Cheese Mini Quiches

12 ounces bacon, chopped

3 cups chopped leeks
(about 3 leeks, white and
light green portions only)

1 1/4 cups half-and-half

2 eggs

2 egg yolks

2 tablespoons minced fresh
thyme leaves

1 teaspoon salt

1/2 teaspoon freshly
ground pepper

1/2 teaspoon nutmeg

1 cup (4 ounces) shredded
extra-sharp Cheddar cheese

2 (16-ounce) packages frozen
puff pastry

Cook the bacon in a medium skillet over medium-high heat for 6 to 8 minutes or until brown and crisp. Remove the bacon with a slotted spoon to paper towels to drain. Drain the skillet, reserving 1 to 2 tablespoons of the bacon drippings in the skillet. Cook the leeks in the reserved bacon drippings over medium heat for 5 minutes or until soft, stirring occasionally. Remove from the heat to cool slightly. Combine the half-and-half, eggs, egg yolks, thyme, salt, pepper and nutmeg in a medium bowl and mix well. Add the cheese, leeks and bacon and mix well.

Position the oven racks in the top and bottom third of the oven. Preheat the oven to 400 degrees. Roll one sheet of the puff pastry at a time into a 10×18-inch rectangle on a lightly floured surface with a floured rolling pin. Cut out 3-inch circles. Save any remaining pastry for another purpose. Press each circle into a miniature muffin cup sprayed with nonstick cooking spray, making sure each circle is centered and that the pastry extends above the top of the cup. Fill each with about 1 tablespoon of the filling. Bake for 20 minutes or until the filling is puffed and the crust is golden brown, switching the position of the muffin pans halfway through baking.

To prepare in advance, freeze the unbaked quiches in the muffin cups for 2 hours or until set. Remove from the muffin cups and place in an airtight container with baking parchment or plastic wrap between each layer or place in a sealed plastic freezer bag. Store in the freezer for up to 1 month. To serve, place the frozen quiches in muffin cups sprayed with nonstick cooking spray. Bake for 30 to 35 minutes or until the filling is puffed and the crust is golden brown.

Makes 4 dozen

LOBSTER QUICHE

1   refrigerator pie pastry
2   cups sliced mushrooms
1   tablespoon olive oil
4   eggs
1   cup heavy cream
1   cup milk
    Dash of cayenne pepper
    Dash of white pepper
    Salt to taste
12   ounces cooked lobster meat
1   cup (4 ounces) shredded
    Gruyère cheese

Preheat the oven to 450 degrees. Line a 9-inch pie plate with the pie pastry, trimming and fluting the edge. Sauté the mushrooms in the olive oil in a skillet for 2 minutes or until tender and brown. Combine the eggs, cream, milk, cayenne pepper, white pepper and salt in a mixing bowl and mix well. Drain the sautéed mushrooms. Layer the sautéed mushrooms, lobster meat and cheese in the pastry-lined pie plate. Pour the egg mixture evenly over the layers. Bake for 10 minutes. Reduce the oven temperature to 350 degrees. Bake for 20 minutes longer or until set.

Serves 8

VEGETABLE QUICHE

1   refrigerator pie pastry
1   cup diagonally sliced carrots
1   cup bite-size broccoli pieces
1   cup bite-size
    cauliflower pieces
4   eggs
1   cup heavy cream
1   cup milk
    Dash of white pepper
    Salt to taste
5   thin slices onion
1/2   cup (2 ounces) shredded
    Pepper Jack cheese
1/2   cup (2 ounces) shredded
    Swiss cheese

Preheat the oven to 350 degrees. Line a 9-inch pie plate with the pie pastry, trimming and fluting the edge. Steam the carrots, broccoli and cauliflower in a steamer basket over boiling water in a saucepan until tender but still very firm; drain. Combine the eggs, cream, milk, white pepper and salt in a mixing bowl and mix well. Arrange the onion slices evenly in the prepared pie plate. Layer the steamed vegetables over the onion slices. Sprinkle with the Pepper Jack cheese and Swiss cheese. Pour the egg mixture over the top. Bake for 1 hour or until a wooden pick inserted in the center comes out clean.

Serves 8

Jalapeño Goat Cheese Frittata

1/2 cup fresh bread crumbs
1 zucchini, thinly sliced
1 large red bell pepper,
   thinly sliced
1 cup sliced fresh mushrooms
8 ounces goat cheese, crumbled
2 tablespoons minced fresh basil
1 or 2 jalapeño chiles, seeded
   and thinly sliced
7 eggs
1/2 cup ricotta cheese
1/2 teaspoon ground pepper
1/4 teaspoon salt

Preheat the oven to 400 degrees. Spray a 10-inch quiche dish with nonstick cooking spray. Sprinkle the bread crumbs evenly in the prepared dish. Bake for 5 minutes or until the bread crumbs are lightly toasted. Remove from the oven to cool. Layer the zucchini, bell pepper, mushrooms, goat cheese, basil and jalapeño chiles over the bread crumbs. Whisk the eggs, cheese, pepper and salt in a bowl until blended. Pour over the layers. Bake for 25 minutes or until set, puffed and light brown. Let stand for 5 minutes before serving.

Serves 6 to 8

Shirred Pancetta and Arugula Eggs

2 slices pancetta

2 tablespoons coarsely
   chopped arugula

2 eggs

   Dash of salt

   Dash of pepper

2 or 3 thin slices Brie cheese

Preheat the oven to 350 degrees. Cover the bottom of a ramekin with the pancetta and sprinkle with the arugula. Crack the eggs over the top. Sprinkle with the salt and pepper. Top with the cheese. Bake for 18 to 20 minutes or until a knife inserted in the center comes out clean and the cheese is light brown.

Serves 1 or 2

Egg Casserole

1 pound link sausage, cut into
   1/2-inch pieces

1/2 green bell pepper, chopped

1/2 red bell pepper, chopped

1/2 onion, chopped

2 tablespoons olive oil

6 slices white bread,
   crusts trimmed

12 eggs

16 ounces Cheddar
    cheese, shredded

11/2 cups milk

1 tablespoon mustard

1 teaspoon Tabasco sauce or
   hot pepper sauce (optional)

Preheat the oven to 300 degrees. Brown the sausage in a skillet. Sauté the bell peppers and onion in the olive oil in a skillet until soft. Arrange the bread in a greased 9×13-inch baking dish. Beat the eggs in a large bowl. Add the sausage, sautéed vegetables, cheese, milk, mustard and Tabasco sauce and mix well. Pour over the bread slices. Bake for 11/2 hours or until set in the middle. Serve with a dollop of sour cream and/or salsa.

Note: This casserole may be assembled and chilled for 8 to 12 hours before baking.

Serves 8

This tasty and easy-to-fix egg casserole is wonderful any time of year, but is especially handy as a holiday morning breakfast as it can be prepared ahead of time. Let it bake while gathering with family and friends, then serve warm with hash browns, fruit, and assorted breads.

SUNDAY EGGS

2   slices rustic bread

2   garlic cloves, cut into halves

    Olive oil for drizzling

6   eggs

1/4   cup milk

1   tablespoon butter

1/2   cup (2 ounces) shredded
    or torn cheese

1/2   cup olive oil

1/4   cup lemon juice

    Salt and pepper to taste

2   cups micro salad greens,
    arugula or spinach

Preheat the broiler. Place the bread in a single layer on a baking sheet. Rub the bread with the garlic. Drizzle with olive oil. Broil until golden and crisp on top.

Beat the eggs and milk in a bowl. Melt the butter in a skillet, swirling to coat the bottom of the skillet. Add the egg mixture and scramble just until set. Fold in the cheese until melted. Do not overcook the eggs. Combine 1/2 cup olive oil, the lemon juice, salt and pepper in a jar with a tight-fitting lid. Seal the jar with the lid and shake well until blended. Pour over the salad greens in a bowl and toss to coat.

To serve, place one slice of bread on each serving plate. Spoon the eggs over the bread. Top with the salad greens. Sprinkle with salt and pepper.

Serves 2

A soon-to-be weekend morning favorite, Sunday Eggs are all about making a delicious and healthy breakfast without muss, fuss, or trips to the grocery store. Prepare with vegetables from your refrigerator that were not used during the week, as well as leftover meats like bacon, pancetta, steak, or sausage and bread from last night's dinner.

Potato, Eggs and Chorizo Tacos

4   red potatoes, cut into
1-inch pieces

1/2   cup water
Salt and pepper to taste

6   chorizo links,
casings removed

8   medium eggs

1/2   cup 1% milk

2   scallions, finely chopped

1   or 2 jalapeño chiles,
finely chopped

12   medium corn tortillas

2   Roma tomatoes, chopped

1/3   cup fresh cilantro

1   cup (4 ounces) shredded
Cotija cheese or jalapeño
Jack cheese

Place the potatoes in a microwave-safe bowl. Add the water. Season with salt and pepper. Microwave, covered with plastic wrap, for 5 minutes. Cook the sausage in a large skillet over medium heat for 5 minutes or until brown, stirring until crumbly. Add the undrained potatoes. Cook for 6 to 8 minutes or until the potatoes are brown and the sausage is cooked through. Whisk the eggs and milk together in a large bowl. Add the scallions, jalapeño chiles, salt and pepper and mix well. Add to the sausage mixture. Cook until set, stirring constantly.

To serve, warm the tortillas in a dry skillet over low heat or wrap the tortillas in a clean damp towel and microwave on High for 1 minute. Divide the egg mixture among the warm tortillas. Top with the tomatoes, cilantro and cheese. Serve with sour cream, guacamole, pico de gallo or salsa and refried beans or black beans.

Note: You may remove the seeds from the jalapeño chiles for less heat, if desired.

Serves 6

CHILE RELLENO CASSEROLE

2   (7-ounce) cans diced green chiles
16 ounces Cheddar cheese, shredded
16 ounces Monterey Jack cheese, shredded
4   eggs, separated
1   (13-ounce) can evaporated milk
3   tablespoons all-purpose flour
2   pinches of salt
2   pinches of pepper
2   (8-ounce) cans tomato sauce

Preheat the oven to 325 degrees. Layer one can of the green chiles, the Cheddar cheese, the remaining can of green chiles and then the Monterey Jack cheese evenly in a 9×13-inch baking pan sprayed with nonstick cooking spray. Beat the egg whites in a mixing bowl until stiff peaks form. Beat the egg yolks, evaporated milk, flour, salt and pepper in a mixing bowl until smooth. Fold in the egg whites. Pour over the layers. Bake for 45 minutes. Pour the tomato sauce over the top. Bake for 30 minutes longer.

Serves 6 to 8

ZUCCHINI SAUSAGE SQUARES

12   ounces bulk pork sausage
1/2 cup chopped onion
4   eggs
1/2 cup (2 ounces) grated Parmesan cheese
18   butter crackers, crushed
1   teaspoon dried basil
1/2 teaspoon oregano
1/8 teaspoon pepper
1   garlic clove, minced
1   pound zucchini, shredded
1   cup (4 ounces) shredded sharp Cheddar cheese

Preheat the oven to 350 degrees. Brown the sausage with the onion in a skillet, stirring until the sausage is crumbly; drain. Whisk the eggs in a medium bowl until blended. Stir in the Parmesan cheese, crackers, basil, oregano, pepper, garlic, zucchini and sausage mixture. Spoon into a greased 9×9-inch baking dish, smoothing the top. Bake for 25 minutes. Top with the Cheddar cheese. Bake for 15 minutes longer or until set in the middle. Cool slightly and cut into squares.

Note: May be assembled and chilled for 8 to 12 hours until ready to bake.

Serves 8 to 10

SALMON AND GRITS

1/2 tablespoon butter

3/4 cup sliced baby bella
mushrooms (optional)

1/4 cup drained capers

2 or 3 garlic cloves, minced

1 large Roma tomato,
chopped (optional)

1/4 cup dry white wine

1 cup plus 2 tablespoons
heavy cream
Salt and pepper to taste

1 3/4 cups half-and-half

3/4 cup water

1/4 teaspoon salt

1/2 cup instant grits

1 cup (4 ounces) shredded
Monterey Jack cheese

4 (8-ounce) skinless
salmon fillets

1 tablespoon olive oil

Melt the butter in a medium heavy saucepan over medium heat. Add the mushrooms and sauté for 5 minutes. Add the capers, garlic and tomato. Sauté for 1 minute or until the garlic begins to change color. Add the wine. Simmer for 1 minute or until the mixture is reduced by one-half. Stir in the cream and bring to a boil. Reduce the heat to medium. Simmer for 10 to 15 minutes or until the sauce thickens, stirring frequently. Sprinkle with salt and pepper to taste.

Bring the half-and-half, water and 1/4 teaspoon salt to a boil in a large heavy saucepan. Whisk in the grits gradually. Reduce the heat to medium-low. Cook, covered, for 6 minutes or until thickened, stirring occasionally. Add the cheese. Cook until melted and smooth, stirring constantly. Season with salt and pepper to taste. Remove from the heat.

Brush the salmon with the olive oil. Sprinkle with salt and pepper to taste. Heat a large heavy skillet over medium-high heat. Place the salmon in the hot skillet. Cook for 4 minutes on each side or until opaque in the center.

To serve, place the grits in the center of each of four shallow bowls. Spoon some of the caper sauce around the grits. Top the grits with the remaining sauce and salmon.

Note: You may stir the juice of 1 large lemon into the sauce after cooking to counteract some of the creaminess. You may use smoked salmon for the fresh.

Serves 4

FRENCH TOAST WITH PECANS

1 loaf rustic bread

8 eggs

2 cups half-and-half

1 teaspoon vanilla extract

1/2 teaspoon nutmeg

1/2 teaspoon cinnamon

1/2 teaspoon mace

3/4 cup (1 1/2 sticks) butter, softened

1 1/3 cups packed brown sugar

3 tablespoons dark corn syrup

1 1/3 cups chopped pecans

Cut the bread into slices. Cut each bread slice into halves. Layer the bread in a heavily buttered 9×13-inch baking pan to within 1/2 inch of the top of the pan. Combine the eggs, half-and-half, vanilla, nutmeg, cinnamon and mace in a bowl and mix well. Pour over the bread. Chill, covered, for 8 to 12 hours.

Preheat the oven to 350 degrees. Combine the butter, brown sugar, corn syrup and pecans in a bowl and mix well. Spoon over the bread mixture. Bake for 50 minutes, tenting with foil halfway after 25 minutes..

Serves 8

RASPBERRY PANCAKES

Raspberry Compote

18	ounces fresh raspberries
1/4	cup sugar
	Zest and juice of 1 lemon

Whipped Cream

1	pint (2 cups) heavy whipping cream
	Vanilla extract to taste
	Confectioners' sugar to taste

Pancakes

4	egg whites
1/4	cup sugar
1	cup ricotta cheese
4	egg yolks
3/4	cup buttermilk
1	cup all-purpose flour
1 1/2	teaspoons baking powder
	Pinch of salt
1/2	cup fresh raspberries
3	tablespoons unsalted butter

For the compote, place the raspberries, sugar, lemon zest and lemon juice in a medium saucepan. Cook over medium heat for 2 minutes or until the sugar dissolves. Remove from the heat and keep warm until serving time.

For the whipped cream, beat the whipping cream in a mixing bowl until frothy. Add vanilla and confectioners' sugar and beat until firm peaks form.

For the pancakes, beat the egg whites and sugar in a mixing bowl until stiff peaks form. Whisk the ricotta cheese and egg yolks together in a large bowl. Whisk in the buttermilk. Sift in the flour, baking powder and salt and whisk just until combined. Fold in the egg whites in two batches. Fold in the raspberries. Melt some of the butter on a hot griddle over medium-low heat. Pour the batter 1/4 cup at a time onto the hot griddle. Cook for 3 minutes on each side or until puffed and golden brown. Top with additional butter, warm raspberry compote and whipped cream. Great served with maple syrup bacon.

Serves 4

These pancakes are equally delicious when blueberries, peaches, cherries, or apricots are substituted for the raspberries.

BANANA PANCAKES

1 2/3   cups all-purpose flour
  2   tablespoons sugar
  1   tablespoon baking powder
3/4   teaspoon salt
1 3/4   cups milk
  2   eggs
1/3   cup butter or
      margarine, melted
  2   or 3 very ripe bananas,
      mashed

Sift the flour, sugar, baking powder and salt into a bowl. Beat the milk and eggs in a bowl until blended. Pour over the flour mixture. Add the butter and beat until blended. Stir in the bananas. Pour 1/4 cup of the batter at a time onto a greased griddle. Cook until bubbles appear on the surface and the underside is golden brown. Turn the pancakes. Cook until golden brown. Place on serving plates. Garnish with chocolate chips. Serve hot with or without syrup.

Serves 4 to 6

BUTTERMILK SYRUP

1 1/2   cups sugar
3/4   cup buttermilk
1/2   cup (1 stick) butter
  2   tablespoons corn syrup
  1   teaspoon baking soda
  2   teaspoons vanilla extract

Combine the sugar, buttermilk, butter, corn syrup and baking soda in a saucepan and mix well. Bring to a boil. Cook for 7 minutes. Remove from the heat. Stir in the vanilla. Store in a jar with a tight-fitting lid in the refrigerator for up to 1 week.

Makes about 2 1/2 cups

PERFECT WAFFLES

1 1/3   cups steel-cut oats
1/2   cup cottage cheese
4   egg whites
1   teaspoon vanilla extract
2   teaspoons olive oil
1   teaspoon baking powder
1   scoop cake batter-flavored
    or vanilla-flavored
    protein powder
1   cup water

Preheat the waffle iron. Grind the oats in a blender. Add the cottage cheese, egg whites, vanilla, olive oil, baking powder, protein powder and 1/2 cup of the water and process until smooth. Add enough of the remaining water gradually until of the desired consistency, processing constantly. Pour about 1/3 cup at a time onto the greased hot waffle iron. Cook using the manufacturer's directions until medium brown.

Note: Reduce the cooking time if you desire to store the waffles in the freezer and reheat later.

Serves 6 to 8

WAFFLES DELUXE

2   cups all-purpose flour
1   tablespoon baking powder
1   teaspoon baking soda
4   eggs
2   cups buttermilk
1/2   cup (1 stick) butter, melted

Preheat the waffle iron. Sift the flour, baking powder and baking soda together into a large bowl. Beat the eggs in a bowl until foamy. Add the buttermilk and butter. Add to the flour mixture and stir just until smooth. Cook in a waffle iron using the manufacturer's directions.

Serves 6

Cottage cheese, steel-cut oats, and protein powder—on their own, each makes a healthy addition to any breakfast. Adding these ingredients to your batter creates healthy and protein-rich waffles everyone will love.

For a more indulgent breakfast, try the Waffles Deluxe. Top with real whipped cream and berries or any seasonal fruit for a restaurant-quality sweet treat. The Buttermilk Syrup recipe on page 24 complements the flavors of these tasty waffles.

PEACH SCONES

1 3/4 cups all-purpose flour
1/3 cup sugar
1 teaspoon baking powder
1/2 teaspoon baking soda
2/3 cup buttermilk
1/3 cup butter, melted
1/2 cup chopped fresh peaches

Preheat the oven to 400 degrees. Mix the flour, sugar, baking powder and baking soda in a bowl. Stir in the buttermilk, butter and peaches just until moistened. Spoon the dough into eight equal mounds 1 to 2 inches apart on a greased 12×15-inch baking sheet. Bake for 15 to 20 minutes or until brown.

Note: Blueberries, apricots, and other fruits and berries may be used instead of the peaches.

Serves 8

WALNUT SHORTCAKE BISCUITS

2 cups all-purpose flour or your flour of choice
1/2 teaspoon salt
4 teaspoons baking powder
1/2 teaspoon baking soda
1/3 cup canola oil
3/4 cup soy milk
2 tablespoons honey
2 teaspoons vanilla extract
1/3 cup chopped walnuts

Preheat the oven to 450 degrees. Place the flour, salt, baking powder and baking soda in a food processor. Mix the canola oil, soy milk, honey and vanilla in a bowl. Add to the flour mixture gradually, processing constantly until a dough is formed and the mixture is no longer crumbly. Stir in the walnuts. Drop by spoonfuls onto a greased baking sheet. Bake for 10 to 15 minutes or until golden brown.

Note: For neat, round biscuits, roll the dough on a lightly floured surface and cut into circles.

Makes about 1 dozen

Serve Walnut Shortcake Biscuits in the morning with butter, honey, or fig jam. These biscuits also make a savory appetizer when paired with blue cheese and bacon. Substitute walnuts with almonds, pecans, or pistachios to create your own variation.

ALMOND BISCOTTI

2 1/2 cups all-purpose flour
3/4 cup chopped almonds
1/2 teaspoon baking powder
1 1/2 cups sugar
1/4 teaspoon salt
1 tablespoon lemon zest
3 eggs
1/2 cup (1 stick) butter, softened
2 teaspoons almond extract
1 egg white, lightly beaten

Preheat the oven to 375 degrees. Mix the flour, almonds, baking powder, sugar, salt and lemon zest in a small bowl. Cream the eggs, butter and almond extract in a mixing bowl until smooth. Add the flour mixture gradually, beating constantly. The dough will be sticky. Divide the dough into two equal portions. Shape each portion into a 3×12-inch log on a silicone-lined baking sheet. Brush the top of each log with the egg white using a pastry brush. Bake for 25 minutes. Remove from the oven. Reduce the oven temperature to 325 degrees. Cut each log diagonally into 1/2-inch slices. Lay cut side down on the silicone-lined baking sheet. Bake for 10 to 12 minutes or until dry. Cool on a wire rack. Store in an airtight container.

Makes 3 dozen

CHOCOLATE ZUCCHINI BREAD

3 large eggs
2 cups packed brown sugar
1 cup vegetable oil
2 cups grated zucchini
1 tablespoon vanilla extract
3 cups all-purpose flour
1 teaspoon baking powder
1 teaspoon salt
1 teaspoon baking soda
1 teaspoon ground allspice
2 teaspoons cinnamon
2 cups (12 ounces) semisweet chocolate chips

Preheat the oven to 325 degrees. Beat the eggs and brown sugar in a mixing bowl until smooth. Add the oil, zucchini and vanilla and mix well. Add the flour, baking powder, salt, baking soda, allspice and cinnamon and beat until smooth. Stir in the chocolate chips. Divide evenly between two greased 5×9-inch loaf pans. Bake for 1 hour or until wooden picks inserted in the centers come out clean. Cool in the pans for 10 minutes. Loosen the edges from the sides of the pans with a knife and invert onto wire racks to cool. Cut into slices.

Note: The loaves can be placed in freezer bags and frozen for up to 2 months. Freeze any additional zucchini to use in this recipe. Place 2 cups grated zucchini in a freezer bag and seal the bag. Freeze for up to 6 months. Thaw the zucchini before using. There will be a lot of liquid, but use the entire contents of the bag in the recipe.

Makes 2 loaves

Hazelnut Zucchini Bread

1   cup hazelnuts, chopped

3   cups unbleached
    all-purpose flour

1   teaspoon salt

1   teaspoon baking soda

1/2   teaspoon baking powder

1   tablespoon cinnamon

1   teaspoon nutmeg

3   eggs

1 3/4   cups granulated sugar

2/3   cup light vegetable oil

3   zucchini, grated
    (about 2 1/2 cups)

1   tablespoon vanilla extract

3   tablespoons hazelnut oil

1   or 2 pinches turbinado sugar
    or natural sugar

Preheat the oven to 350 degrees. Spread the hazelnuts on a baking sheet. Bake for 8 to 10 minutes or until toasted. Maintain the oven temperature.

Sift the flour, salt, baking soda, baking powder, cinnamon and nutmeg together. Beat the eggs in a mixing bowl until pale yellow. Add the granulated sugar and mix well. Add the vegetable oil, zucchini and vanilla and mix well. Stir in the flour mixture 1 cup at a time. Add the toasted hazelnuts and hazelnut oil and mix well. Spoon into two buttered 5×9-inch loaf pans. Sprinkle the tops with the specialty sugar. Bake for 45 minutes or until the loaves test done. Invert onto wire racks to cool.

Note: The bread may be baked in four small loaf pans.

Makes 2 loaves

CHUNKY MONKEY CINNAMON BREAD

1/2 cup nonfat dry milk powder

1/3 cup granulated sugar

2 teaspoons dry yeast

33/4 cups all-purpose flour

1/4 teaspoon baking powder

1/4 teaspoon baking soda

1 teaspoon salt

11/3 cups hot water

1/3 cup vegetable oil

1/2 cup (1 stick) butter, melted

1 cup granulated sugar

1 tablespoon cinnamon

1 cup packed brown sugar

Line two 9-inch loaf pans with baking parchment, allowing enough to hang over the edges. Combine the dry milk powder, 1/3 cup granulated sugar, the yeast, 31/2 cups of the flour, the baking powder, baking soda and salt in the bowl of a stand mixer fitted with a dough hook. Beat, covered, until well mixed. Add the hot water and oil. Beat at the lowest speed until barely mixed, scraping down the side of the bowl. Add enough of the remaining 1/4 cup flour 1 tablespoon at a time until the dough leaves the side of the bowl, beating at medium-low speed.

Place the dough on a lightly floured surface. Knead for 1 to 2 minutes or until smooth and elastic. Shape into a round ball. Place in an oiled bowl, turning to coat the surface. Let rise, covered with plastic wrap, for 1 to 11/2 hours or until doubled in bulk.

Place the dough on a work surface, adding additional oil if needed to prevent the dough from sticking to the surface. Roll into an 18×24-inch rectangle 1/2 inch thick. Spread generously with some of the melted butter to the edges with a spatula. Sprinkle generously with a mixture of 1 cup granulated sugar and the cinnamon. Cover generously with the brown sugar. Roll loosely to enclose the filling. Cut at a 45-degree angle into 1-inch slices using a dough scraper. Cut each slice diagonally in the other direction in an "X" pattern. You may coarsely chop the dough a few more times, if desired.

Pour some of the remaining butter into the bottom of each prepared pan. Divide the chopped dough evenly among the pans. Drizzle the remaining butter over the loaves. Sprinkle with the remaining cinnamon-sugar mixture. Let rise for 1 to 11/2 hours or until doubled in bulk.

Preheat the oven to 350 degrees. Bake for 30 to 40 minutes or until the bread tests done in the center. Let stand for 10 minutes. Remove to wire racks to cool completely.

Makes 2 loaves

APPLE PECAN STREUSEL MUFFINS

1/2 cup chopped pecans

6 tablespoons brown sugar

1 teaspoon cinnamon

2 cups unbleached all-purpose flour or white whole wheat flour

1/2 cup whole wheat flour

3/4 cup natural cane sugar

1 teaspoon baking powder

1 teaspoon baking soda

1/2 teaspoon ground cloves

1 teaspoon cinnamon

1/2 teaspoon sea salt

1/2 cup soy milk or milk

1/2 cup applesauce

2 eggs, beaten

1/4 cup (1/2 stick) unsalted butter, melted

1 teaspoon vanilla extract

2 cups finely chopped peeled apples

Preheat the oven to 350 degrees. Mix the pecans, brown sugar and 1 teaspoon cinnamon in a small bowl. Mix the all-purpose flour, whole wheat flour, cane sugar, baking powder, baking soda, cloves, 1 teaspoon cinnamon and the sea salt in a mixing bowl. Whisk the soy milk, applesauce, eggs, butter and vanilla in a bowl until smooth. Add to the flour mixture and stir until moistened. Fold in the apples. Spoon into nonstick muffin cups, filling a little over half-full. Sprinkle the pecan mixture evenly over the batter. Bake for 20 minutes or until the muffins spring back when lightly touched. Remove the muffins immediately to wire racks to cool or serve warm.

Makes 1 dozen

BLUEBERRY CRUMBLE MUFFINS

Topping

1/3	cup sugar
1/3	cup all-purpose flour
1/4	teaspoon salt
1/4	teaspoon cinnamon
3	tablespoons unsalted butter, melted

For the topping, combine the sugar, flour, salt, cinnamon and butter in a bowl and rub together with your fingertips until crumbly.

Muffins

2	cups all-purpose flour
1	tablespoon baking powder
1/2	teaspoon salt
1/2	cup sugar
1	egg
1/2	cup milk
1/2	cup sour cream
1/3	cup unsalted butter, melted
2	teaspoons lemon juice
1	teaspoon grated lemon zest
1 1/2	cups fresh blueberries

For the muffins, preheat the oven to 400 degrees. Sift the flour, baking powder, salt and sugar into a large bowl. Combine the egg, milk, sour cream, butter, lemon juice and lemon zest in a bowl and mix well. Add to the flour mixture and stir until moistened. Fold in the blueberries. Fill twelve paper-lined muffin cups full. Crumble the topping over the muffin batter and press gently to adhere. Bake for 20 minutes or until light brown.

Note: Try using chopped Bing cherries, black cherries, fresh raspberries, chopped nectarines, chopped fresh peaches or huckleberries instead of the blueberries with or without the crumb topping.

Makes 1 dozen

Nutty Honey Granola

1/2 cup honey

1/2 cup packed light or dark
    brown sugar

1 1/2 teaspoons vanilla extract

2 cups old-fashioned
    rolled oats

1 cup sunflower seeds

1 cup slivered almonds

1 cup walnuts or pecans

1 cup shredded coconut

Photograph at left.

Preheat the oven to 325 degrees. Heat the honey and brown sugar in a small saucepan over low heat until the brown sugar melts. Remove from the heat. Stir in the vanilla.

Mix the oats, sunflower seeds, almonds, walnuts and coconut in a large bowl. Add the brown sugar mixture and toss to coat evenly. Spread evenly on a silicone-lined rimmed baking sheet. Bake for 30 to 35 minutes or until evenly brown, stirring once or twice. Remove from the oven to cool completely. Break the granola into chunks and store in a sealable plastic bag or airtight container.

Note: Any combination of nuts may be used. Feel free to substitute macadamia nuts, cashews, or pumpkin seeds.

Serves 14

Greek Yogurt, Honey and Poppy Seeds with Blackberries

12 ounces plain Greek yogurt

3 tablespoons honey

2 1/2 tablespoons fresh lemon juice

1 1/2 teaspoons poppy seeds

1/4 teaspoon vanilla extract

2 to 4 packages blackberries

Combine the yogurt, honey, lemon juice, poppy seeds and vanilla in a bowl and mix well. Drizzle over the blackberries in a serving bowl.

Serves 6 to 8

FRESH FRUIT WITH ORANGE CREAM

1 pint strawberries, sliced
   apples, oranges, bananas or
   mixed berries

1/2 cup plus 1 tablespoon sugar

2 teaspoons grated
   orange zest

1/2 cup orange juice

1 cup heavy whipping cream

Rinse the strawberries. Toss the strawberries with 1 tablespoon of the sugar in a bowl.

Mix the remaining 1/2 cup sugar, the orange zest and orange juice in a small saucepan. Bring to a boil, stirring until the sugar dissolves. Reduce the heat and simmer for 10 minutes or until the mixture begins to thicken. Remove from the heat and let stand until cool. Whip the whipping cream in a mixing bowl until firm peaks form. Fold in the orange syrup. Garnish with chopped toasted almonds. Serve with the strawberries or other fresh fruit for dipping.

Note: For mini parfait cups, place a few berries in parfait cups and drizzle the orange cream over the top. Garnish with mint leaves.

Serves 6 to 8

FRESH FRUIT SALAD

8 ounces blueberries

8 ounces strawberries, thinly
   sliced lengthwise

8 ounces raspberries

3 large bananas, thinly sliced

1 cup confectioners' sugar
   Juice of 1 orange
   Juice of 1/2 lemon

Combine the blueberries, strawberries, raspberries and bananas in a medium salad bowl. Combine the confectioners' sugar, orange juice and lemon juice in a small mixing bowl and stir until the confectioners' sugar is dissolved. Pour over the fruit and serve.

Serves 4 to 6

LIME RUM MARINATED FRUIT

1 honeydew melon

1 cantaloupe

1 cup sugar

1/3 cup water

2 teaspoons grated lime zest

6 tablespoons fresh lime juice
(juice of 2 or 3 limes)

1/2 cup clear rum

1 pint fresh raspberries

1 1/2 tablespoons chopped
fresh mint

Cut the honeydew melon and cantaloupe into chunks and place in a serving bowl. Bring the sugar and water to a boil in a saucepan. Reduce the heat and simmer for 5 minutes. Stir in the lime zest. Remove from the heat to cool. Stir in the lime juice and rum. Pour over the fruit and toss to coat. Chill for several hours. Add the raspberries just before serving. Sprinkle with the mint. Garnish with additional lime zest.

Note: The marinade can be used with any type of melon or sturdy fruit such as fresh pineapple. More delicate fruit can be added just before serving.

Serves 8

MILLER'S BASIC HONEY BUTTER WITH VARIATIONS

1 cup (2 sticks) butter, softened

1/3 cup Miller's clover honey

Mix the butter and honey in a bowl until smooth. Store in the refrigerator or freezer.

Note: Increase the honey to 1/2 cup for sweeter honey butter.

The Beehive State's first local honey company, Miller's Honey, started in 1894 when Nephi Ephraim Miller traded five bags of oats for seven colonies of bees. Since that time, three generations of the Miller family have produced an abundance of fine honeys, ranging from the more common types like clover, alfalfa, and wildflower to the rarer varieties like avocado, eucalyptus, and Hawaiian blossom.

Variations:

For Almond Honey Butter, add 1 tablespoon almond extract.

For Spiced Honey Butter, add 1 tablespoon pumpkin pie spice.

For Cinnamon Honey Butter, add 1 tablespoon cinnamon.

For Lemon Honey Butter, add 1 teaspoon grated lemon zest.

For Orange Honey Butter, add 1 teaspoon grated orange zest.

For Bavarian Honey Butter, increase the honey to 1/2 cup and add 1/2 cup whipping cream and 1 teaspoon vanilla extract.

Serves 16

Sips & Snacks

Papaya Colada 38 • Pink Grapefruit Sparkling Sangria 38 • Margaritas 39
Raspberry Mojito 39 • The Phil Collins Drink 40 • Pomtini 40
Pimm's Treat with Homemade Lemonade 41 • Champagne Cosmopolitan 43
Hot Cranberry Punch 43 • Asian Meatballs with Soy Honey Ginger Sauce 44 • Pot Stickers 45
Chinese Chicken Wings 46 • Sassy Shrimp 46 • Skewered Shrimp with Peanut Dipping Sauce 47
Marguerite Henderson's Grilled Herbed Shrimp 49 • Deviled Eggs with Tarragon and Watercress 50
Cheese-Stuffed Mushrooms 50 • Gorgonzola-Stuffed Dates 51
Sage and Prosciutto Popovers 51 • Beer, Basil and Asiago Bread 52 • Cheesy Artichoke Cups 53
Mexican Won Tons 53 • Fava Bean Crostini 55 • Apple Fontina Bites 55
Corn Cakes with Peach Mustard Sauce 56 • Polenta Pesto Squares 57
Utah's Own Arugula Pesto 57 • Party Turnovers 58 • Black Pepper Almonds 59
White Pepper Cashews 59 • Sweet-and-Spicy Nuts 60 • Camembert Cheese Crisps 60
Baked Goat Cheese 61 • Amaretto and Brie Cheese 61
Holiday Cranberry Chutney with Brie Cheese 63 • Hell's Backbone Grill Goat Cheese Fondue 64
Crab Meat Spread 65 • White Bean Hummus 65 • Blue Cheese Chicken Wing Dip 66
Clam Dip 66 • Greek Layered Dip 67 • Green Goddess Dip 67 • Yogurt Onion Dip 68
Cranberry Jalapeño Salsa 68 • Mango Salsa 69 • Real Salt Chips 69

Papaya Colada

1/4 to 1/2 cup cream of coconut

1/2 cup pineapple juice

1 papaya, chopped

1/2 cup ice

1/2 cup rum

2 to 3 tablespoons canned whipped cream

Process the cream of coconut, pineapple juice, papaya, ice, rum and whipped cream in a blender until smooth. Pour into serving glasses.

Serves 4

Pink Grapefruit Sparkling Sangria

2 small pink grapefruit, sliced

2 ounces lemonade

2 ounces Grand Marnier or Chambord

2 tablespoons sugar

1 (750-milliliter) bottle sparkling wine

Mix the grapefruit slices, lemonade, liqueur and sugar in a large glass pitcher. Muddle the mixture with a long-handled spoon to release the fruit juices. Stir until the sugar dissolves. Chill for 2 hours. Stir in the sparkling wine gradually with a long-handled spoon just before serving. Fill serving glasses with ice cubes. Pour the sangria over the ice, allowing the fruit slices to fall into the glasses.

Serves 8

To make a refreshing non-alcoholic grapefruit sangria, substitute sparkling water for sparkling wine and use the juice from half an orange in place of the Grand Marnier.

MARGARITAS

6 ounces pink grapefruit juice
  or raspberry lemonade
3 ounces tequila
2 ounces Grand Marnier
1 ounce lime juice
6 ounces sweet-and-sour mix
2 ounces Midori or blue curaçao
2 limes, cut into wedges

Mix the pink grapefruit juice, tequila, Grand Marnier, lime juice, sweet-and-sour mix and curaçao in a pitcher. Pour over crushed ice in margarita glasses and add the lime wedges.

Serves 2 or 3

RASPBERRY MOJITO

3 or 4 sprigs of fresh mint
8 raspberries
2 teaspoons sugar
1 1/2 ounces white rum
2 ounces fresh lime juice
  Soda water to taste

Muddle the mint, raspberries and sugar in a tall glass until mixed and fragrant. Add the rum and lime juice and mix well. Add a handful of ice cubes. Top with soda water. Garnish with a sprig of fresh mint and 2 or 3 raspberries.

Serves 1

The Phil Collins Drink

2 thin slices cucumber

3 large mint leaves

Juice from 1 lemon slice

2 ounces limeade

2 ounces gin

2 ounces club soda

Place the cucumber and mint in a shaker. Top with ice cubes, the lemon juice and 1 ounce of the limeade and muddle well. Add enough ice cubes to fill the shaker halfway. Add the remaining 1 ounce limeade and gin and shake well. Pour into a tall glass and add more ice if needed. Stir in the club soda. Garnish with a sprig of fresh mint and a lime slice.

Serves 1

Pomtini

1 ounce pomegranate juice

1 1/2 ounces vodka

1 1/2 ounces grapefruit juice

1/2 ounce fresh lime juice

1/2 ounce simple syrup

Combine the pomegranate juice, vodka, grapefruit juice, lime juice and simple syrup with ice cubes in a shaker and shake well. Strain into a chilled martini glass.

Serves 1

Pimm's Treat with Homemade Lemonade

Homemade Lemonade

1   cup sugar

2   cups water

1   cup fresh lemon juice

Pimm's Treat

2   ounces gin, such as
    Hendricks cucumber gin

2   ounces Pimm's No. 1 Cup
    Lemon-lime soda

For the lemonade, simmer the sugar and 1 cup of the water in a saucepan until the sugar dissolves. Remove from the heat to cool. Combine the simple syrup, remaining 1 cup of water and lemon juice in a pitcher and mix well. Store in the refrigerator.

For the Pimm's Treat, pour the gin, liqueur and 4 ounces of the lemonade into a pitcher and mix well, reserving the remaining lemonade for another purpose. Add the ice and a splash of the soda. Pour into tall glasses. Garnish with thin cucumber slices.

Serves 2

CHAMPAGNE COSMOPOLITAN

1 cup Cointreau

1 cup cranberry juice cocktail

1/2 cup fresh lime juice

2 tablespoons superfine sugar

2 (750-milliliter) bottles
Champagne or other
sparkling wine

Photograph at left.

Mix the Cointreau, cranberry juice cocktail, lime juice and sugar in a small pitcher and mix well. Chill, covered, for 2 to 4 hours. Stir the juice mixture. Place 2 to 3 tablespoons of the juice mixture in a martini glass. Add enough Champagne to fill the glass.

Serves 8 to 10

HOT CRANBERRY PUNCH

2 cups water

1 1/2 cups sugar

4 cinnamon sticks

1 quart (4 cups) cranberry
juice cocktail

1 quart (4 cups) water

2 cups orange juice

2 tablespoons lemon juice

Simmer 2 cups water, the sugar and cinnamon sticks in a saucepan for 10 minutes. Stir in the cranberry juice, 1 quart water, the orange juice and lemon juice. Simmer for 30 minutes. Ladle into serving cups.

Serves 10 to 12

ASIAN MEATBALLS WITH
SOY HONEY GINGER SAUCE

Soy Honey Ginger Sauce

- 1/4 cup soy sauce
- 1/4 cup honey
- 1/4 cup water
- 1 teaspoon Asian chili sauce
- 1/4 cup scallions
- 1 teaspoon ginger
- 1/4 teaspoon cornstarch

Meatballs

- 1 egg
- 2 tablespoons soy sauce
- 1 garlic clove, minced
- 1/4 cup chopped scallions
- 1 tablespoon sesame oil
- 1 teaspoon Asian chili sauce
- 1 cup water chestnuts, chopped
- 1 cup panko (Japanese bread crumbs)
- 1 pound ground turkey
- 2 tablespoons water
- 1/2 cup vegetable oil

For the sauce, bring the soy sauce, honey, water, chili sauce, scallions and ginger to a boil in a saucepan. Reduce the heat and simmer for 3 to 5 minutes or until the sauce is reduced. Stir in the cornstarch. Cook until slightly thickened, stirring constantly. Keep warm.

For the meatballs, mix the egg, soy sauce, garlic, scallions, sesame oil, chili sauce, water chestnuts and panko with a fork in a bowl. Add the ground turkey and mix well. Add the water 1 tablespoon at a time, mixing well after each addition until the desired degree of moistness. Shape into 1-inch balls. Heat the oil in a large sauté pan. Add the meatballs, being careful not to overcrowd the pan. Fry for 1 to 2 minutes on each side until brown and cooked through. Remove the meatballs to a platter lined with paper towels to drain. Serve warm with the sauce.

Note: The meatballs may be baked instead of fried. Preheat the oven to 400 degrees. Place the meatballs in a baking pan sprayed with nonstick cooking spray. Bake for 30 to 40 minutes or until cooked through. Preheat the broiler. Broil for 3 to 5 minutes or until brown.

Serves 10

POT STICKERS

1 pound ground pork, chicken or turkey

1 egg

3/4 cup finely chopped fresh shiitake mushroom caps

3/4 cup minced Napa cabbage

1/2 cup water chestnuts, chopped

1/2 cup minced scallions

2 garlic cloves, minced

1 tablespoon cornstarch

2 teaspoons grated fresh ginger

3 tablespoons soy sauce

1 tablespoon oyster sauce

2 tablespoons dry white wine or gin

1/2 teaspoon sugar

Salt to taste

1/4 teaspoon white pepper

60 square pot sticker wrappers

3 tablespoons vegetable oil

1 cup water

Mix the ground pork, egg, mushrooms, cabbage, water chestnuts, scallions, garlic, cornstarch, ginger, soy sauce, oyster sauce, wine, sugar, salt and white pepper in a bowl.

Fill a small bowl with water. Place a scant 1 tablespoon of the filling in the center of one wrapper. Dip your fingers in the water and moisten the edges of the wrapper. Bring the opposite edges together over the filling and pinch together in the center. Make two pleats on each side of the center, folding to the center and pressing all edges to seal. Place seam side up on a lightly floured baking sheet and cover with plastic wrap. Repeat with the remaining filling and wrappers.

Preheat the oven to 200 degrees. Coat the bottom of a 12-inch nonstick skillet with 1 tablespoon of the oil. Arrange one-third of the pot stickers seam side up and slightly apart in a single layer in the hot skillet. Cook over medium-high heat for 3 to 5 minutes or until the bottoms are golden brown. Add 1/3 cup of the water. Cover the skillet tightly. Reduce the heat to medium-low. Cook for 4 to 6 minutes or until firm to the touch. Uncover and continue to cook over medium-high heat until the liquid evaporates. Place on a baking sheet and keep warm in the preheated oven. Repeat with the remaining pot stickers, oil and water.

Serves 15

CHINESE CHICKEN WINGS

3/4 cup orange juice

1 (5-ounce) bottle soy sauce

1/4 cup packed brown sugar

2 garlic cloves, crushed

1 or 2 dashes of ginger

3 to 5 pounds chicken wings

Mix the orange juice, soy sauce, brown sugar, garlic and ginger in a bowl. Place the chicken wings in a sealable plastic bag. Add the marinade and seal the bag. Marinate in the refrigerator for 8 to 12 hours, turning the bag a couple of times.

Preheat the oven to 350 degrees. Drain the chicken wings, reserving the marinade. Place the chicken wings on a baking sheet. Bake for 45 minutes, basting with the reserved marinade.

Note: For a simple dipping sauce to serve with the chicken wings, mix teriyaki sauce with a dash of Sriracha hot chili sauce.

Serves 6

SASSY SHRIMP

1/4 cup vegetable oil

2 garlic cloves, crushed

1 tablespoon dry mustard

2 teaspoons salt

1/2 cup lemon juice

1 tablespoon red wine vinegar

1 bay leaf, crushed

1/2 teaspoon paprika

Dash of red pepper

1 lemon, thinly sliced

1 red onion, thinly sliced

2 pounds deveined peeled
  cooked shrimp

Combine the oil, garlic, dry mustard, salt, lemon juice, vinegar, bay leaf, paprika and red pepper in a large bowl and mix well. Add the lemon, onion and shrimp and toss to coat. Marinate, covered, in the refrigerator for 2 hours. Garnish with parsley just before serving. Serve slightly chilled or at room temperature.

Serves 6 to 8

Skewered Shrimp with Peanut Dipping Sauce

Peanut Dipping Sauce

2	teaspoons canola oil
4	garlic cloves, pressed
1 1/2	teaspoons red pepper flakes
1	teaspoon hot pepper sauce
1/2	cup hoisin sauce
3	tablespoons creamy peanut butter
1/2	cup water
	Juice of 2 large limes

Skewered Shrimp

36	large shrimp
1	tablespoon hoisin sauce
	Juice of 1 large lime
1	teaspoon grated fresh ginger

For the dipping sauce, heat the canola oil in a small saucepan over medium heat. Add the garlic and sauté for 1 minute. Add the red pepper flakes and hot sauce. Cook for a few seconds, stirring constantly. Stir in the hoisin sauce, peanut butter and water. Reduce the heat to medium-low and simmer gently. Stir in the lime juice. Simmer for 3 to 4 minutes or until the flavors are blended.

For the shrimp, soak twelve short wooden skewers in water to cover in a bowl for 1 hour or longer; drain. Preheat the grill or broiler. Thread three shrimp on each skewer. Mix the hoisin sauce, lime juice and ginger in a small bowl. Brush over both sides of the shrimp skewers. Place on a grill rack or broiler rack. Grill or broil for 3 to 4 minutes or until the shrimp turn pink. Serve with the dipping sauce warmed or at room temperature.

Note: You may brush each shrimp with the sauce and grill or broil individually. Serve with wooden picks for dipping into the dipping sauce.

Serves 12

Marguerite Henderson's Grilled Herbed Shrimp

Lemon Aïoli Dipping Sauce

- 1 cup mayonnaise
- 2 garlic cloves, minced
- 1 tablespoon chopped fresh Italian parsley
- 1 teaspoon lemon zest

Shrimp

- 1 pound deveined peeled jumbo shrimp (21 to 26 per pound)
- Zest and juice of 1 large orange
- Zest and juice of 1 large lemon
- 1/2 cup fresh tarragon, dill weed or oregano, chopped
- 1/2 cup fresh Italian parsley, chopped
- 1 teaspoon kosher salt
- 1/4 teaspoon red pepper flakes
- 2 garlic cloves, minced
- 2 tablespoons olive oil

For the sauce, combine the mayonnaise, garlic, parsley and lemon zest in a bowl and mix well.

For the shrimp, combine the shrimp, orange zest, orange juice, lemon zest, lemon juice, tarragon, parsley, kosher salt, red pepper flakes, garlic and olive oil in a large bowl and toss to coat. Marinate, covered, in the refrigerator for up to 4 hours. Drain the shrimp, discarding the marinade. Preheat the grill. Place the shrimp in a single layer in a grill basket. Grill over medium heat for 3 to 4 minutes and turn. Continue grilling until the shrimp turn pink; do not overcook. Thread the shrimp on decorative skewers or wooden picks. Serve with the dipping sauce.

Serves 4 to 6

This versatile dish is prepared as an appetizer with Lemon Aïoli Dipping Sauce. It can also be combined with a variety of greens for a hearty salad, or paired with rice for a satisfying entrée.

Deviled Eggs with Tarragon and Watercress

12 extra-large eggs

24 fresh tarragon leaves

3/4 cup watercress

4 scallions, chopped

5 to 6 tablespoons mayonnaise

2 teaspoons Dijon mustard

Salt and pepper to taste

Place the eggs in a large saucepan and fill with cold water. Bring to a boil over medium heat. Cook for 10 minutes. Drain the eggs. Add enough cold water to the eggs to cover. Let stand for 30 minutes or until the eggs are cool. Peel the eggs and cut into halves lengthwise. Process the egg yolks in a food processor for 30 to 60 seconds or until smooth. Place the egg yolks in a mixing bowl. Process the tarragon leaves, watercress and scallions in the food processor until the mixture is minced. Add to the egg yolks. Add the mayonnaise, Dijon mustard, salt and pepper and mix well. Spoon into the egg whites and place on a serving platter. Chill for 30 to 60 minutes before serving.

Note: To make Green Deviled Eggs and Ham, place two thin slices of ham into each egg white before adding the egg yolk mixture.

Serves 6 to 8

Cheese-Stuffed Mushrooms

2 pounds fresh large mushrooms

1/2 cup (1 stick) butter, melted

8 ounces cream cheese, softened

1/4 cup cream or half-and-half

3/4 cup (3 ounces) grated Romano cheese or Parmesan cheese

1/2 teaspoon garlic powder

2 tablespoons chopped chives or green onion tops

Parsley flakes to taste

Preheat the oven to 350 degrees. Brush the mushrooms clean and discard the stems. Dip each mushroom cap into the butter, turning to coat thoroughly. Place in a single layer on a baking sheet. Combine the cream cheese, cream, Romano cheese, garlic powder and chives in a medium bowl and mix well. Mound 1 teaspoon of the cheese mixture into each mushroom cap. Sprinkle with parsley flakes. Bake for 15 to 17 minutes or until brown.

Note: These may be prepared ahead and frozen before baking. To serve, place the frozen mushroom caps on a baking sheet and bake as directed above, adding 5 to 7 minutes to the baking time.

Serves 8 to 10

Gorgonzola-Stuffed Dates

12 large dates

1/2 cup gorgonzola cheese

6 slices bacon

Preheat the oven to 375 degrees. Cut the dates lengthwise just enough to remove the pits. Fill the opening with the cheese and press closed. Cut the bacon into halves. Cook in a skillet for 3 to 4 minutes or until still pliable. Remove the bacon to paper towels and blot to remove the grease. Wrap each date with a slice of bacon and secure the ends with a wooden pick. Place on a baking sheet sprayed with nonstick cooking spray. Bake for 12 to 15 minutes or until the dates are puffy and the cheese melts. Serve immediately.

Makes 1 dozen

Sage and Prosciutto Popovers

1 1/2 cups all-purpose flour

1/2 cup milk

1 1/2 teaspoons salt

4 medium eggs

2 tablespoons butter, softened

12 small pats of butter

3 to 4 tablespoons minced fresh sage leaves, or 1 tablespoon dried sage

3 ounces prosciutto, chopped

Mix the flour, milk, salt, eggs and 2 tablespoons butter in a bowl until smooth. Chill in the refrigerator. Preheat the oven to 400 degrees. Place a small pat of butter, the sage and prosciutto in each cup of a 12-cup popover pan or an 18-cup muffin pan. Bake until the butter just begins to sizzle. Remove from the oven and fill each cup two-thirds full with the batter as quickly as possible. Bake for 40 minutes. Pierce the top of each popover quickly with a fork to allow the steam to escape.

Makes 1 dozen

BEER, BASIL AND ASIAGO BREAD

Bread

3 1/2	cups all-purpose flour
2 1/2	teaspoons dry yeast
1 1/2	teaspoons kosher salt
1/2	teaspoon pepper
1	cup chopped fresh basil
1	cup (4 ounces) shredded asiago cheese
1	(12-ounce) bottle pale ale

For the bread, preheat the oven to 400 degrees. Mix the flour, yeast, kosher salt, and pepper with a wooden spoon in a large bowl. Add the basil, cheese and ale and mix to form a soft dough. Shape the dough into a loaf using floured hands. Place on an oiled baking sheet. Bake for 40 to 45 minutes or until a wooden pick inserted in the center comes out clean.

Garlic Butter

1	cup (2 sticks) butter, softened
1	tablespoon garlic salt
1	teaspoon freshly ground pepper
1	teaspoon Italian seasoning

For the garlic butter, combine the butter, garlic salt, pepper and Italian seasoning in a bowl and mix well. Serve with the warm bread.

Makes 1 loaf

Utah's abundance of local artisan beer brewers makes the variations for this recipe almost endless. A light-colored beer such as a pilsner or hefeweizen creates lighter-flavored bread, while a dark beer such as an oatmeal stout or amber ale creates a richer, more robust flavor.

CHEESY ARTICHOKE CUPS

1 (12-ounce) jar marinated
  artichoke hearts
1 (4-ounce) can chopped
  green chiles
2 green onions, chopped
1/4 cup chopped red bell pepper
1/4 cup chopped red onion
1 garlic clove, pressed
1/4 cup (1 ounce) grated
  Parmesan cheese
1/2 cup sour cream
12 (3-inch square) won ton
  wrappers

Preheat the oven to 350 degrees. Drain the artichoke hearts and pat dry with a paper towel. Chop the artichoke hearts. Combine the artichoke hearts, green chiles, green onions, bell pepper, red onion, garlic, cheese and sour cream in a bowl and mix well. Spray twelve muffin cups with nonstick cooking spray. Line each cup with a won ton wrapper. Spoon the artichoke mixture evenly into each cup. Fold the corners of the won ton wrappers over the filling. Bake for 12 to 14 minutes or until brown. Cool in the muffin cups for a few minutes. Remove to a serving platter.

Makes 1 dozen

MEXICAN WON TONS

100 round won ton wrappers
3 (16-ounce) cans spicy
  refried beans
1 or 2 small onions, minced
1 envelope taco seasoning mix
3/4 teaspoon cumin
2 1/2 cups (10 ounces) shredded
  Mexican cheese blend
2 cups sour cream
  Mango Salsa (see page 69)

Preheat the oven to 350 degrees. Line miniature muffin cups with the won ton wrappers. Bake for 7 to 9 minutes or until the edges are golden brown. Combine the beans, onions, taco seasoning mix, cumin and cheese in a bowl and mix well. Fill each won ton wrapper one-half full with the bean mixture. Place on a baking sheet. Bake for 5 to 8 minutes or until heated through. Top each with a dollop of the sour cream and top with the salsa. Garnish with chopped cilantro.

Note: If the salsa is too chunky, pulse in a food processor until of the desired consistency.

Serves 20

Fava Bean Crostini

3 1/2   pounds fresh fava beans,
       shelled (about 4 cups)
2   garlic cloves, minced
2   teaspoons finely
       chopped thyme
2   teaspoons fresh lemon juice
1   teaspoon finely grated
       lemon zest
1   cup extra-virgin olive oil
       Pinch of salt, or to taste
       Pinch of pepper
24   thick slices Italian bread
       Olive oil for drizzling

Photograph at left.

Bring water to a boil in a medium saucepan and add the beans. Place in a bowl of ice water to cool. Drain the beans. Peel and discard the tough outer skins.

Purée the beans, garlic, thyme, lemon juice and lemon zest in a food processor. Add 3/4 cup of the olive oil in a fine stream, processing constantly until smooth. Spoon into a medium bowl. Stir in a pinch of salt and pepper.

Preheat the broiler. Brush the bread on both sides with the remaining 1/4 cup olive oil. Arrange on a baking sheet. Broil 4 inches from the heat source for 1 minute on each side or until golden brown and crisp. Spread with the bean purée and arrange on a serving platter. Drizzle with olive oil. Season to taste with salt. Serve with lemon wedges.

Serves 12 to 15

Apple Fontina Bites

12   slices crostini
1   tablespoon olive oil
1/2   teaspoon granulated sugar
1   tablespoon brown sugar
1   tablespoon minced pecans
12   thin slices gala apple
12   slices fontina cheese

Preheat the oven to 350 degrees. Place the crostini on a lined baking sheet. Brush with the olive oil and sprinkle with the granulated sugar. Bake for 5 minutes. Remove from the oven to cool.

Mix the brown sugar and pecans in a bowl. Arrange the toasted crostini close together on the baking sheet. Top each with a slice of apple and a slice of fontina cheese. Sprinkle with the pecan mixture. Bake for 10 minutes or until the cheese is slightly melted. Serve warm.

Makes 1 dozen

CORN CAKES WITH PEACH MUSTARD SAUCE

Peach Mustard Sauce

3	tablespoons peach or apricot jam
1	teaspoon Dijon mustard
1	teaspoon yellow mustard

Corn Cakes

2 1/2	cups fresh corn kernels (about 5 ears)
3	eggs
3/4	cup milk
3	tablespoons butter, melted
3/4	cup all-purpose flour
3/4	cup yellow or white cornmeal
1	cup (4 ounces) shredded mozzarella cheese
1/4	cup chopped green onion tops
1	teaspoon salt
1	teaspoon ground pepper

For the sauce, mix the jam, Dijon mustard and yellow mustard in a small bowl. Serve with the corn cakes.

For the corn cakes, pulse the corn, eggs, milk and butter in a food processor just until the corn is coarsely chopped. Mix the flour, cornmeal, cheese, green onion tops, salt and pepper in a large bowl. Add the corn mixture and stir until moistened. Spoon about 2 tablespoons of the batter at a time onto a hot greased griddle or in a nonstick skillet, spreading slighting to form 2- to 3-inch cakes. Cook for 3 minutes on each side or until golden brown and cooked through. Do not flatten the cakes once turned.

Serves 6

POLENTA PESTO SQUARES

8　(1/2-inch-thick) squares
　　polenta
8　small lettuce leaves
1/4　cup Utah's Own Arugula
　　Pesto (below)
1/4　cup toasted pine nuts

Place the polenta squares on a large plate. Top each with 1 leaf of lettuce, 1/2 tablespoon of the pesto and 1/2 tablespoon of the pine nuts. Serve with Tea Grotto genmaicha tea.

Serves 8

UTAH'S OWN ARUGULA PESTO

2　cups (1-inch) arugula strips
4　garlic cloves
1/2　cup toasted pepitas
　　(pumpkin seeds)
1/2　cup olive oil
1/2　cup (2 ounces) shredded
　　Beehive Cheese
　　Promontory Cheddar
1/2　teaspoon sea salt
1/2　teaspoon freshly
　　ground pepper
2　tablespoons balsamic vinegar

Process the arugula and garlic in a food processor for 10 seconds. Add the pepitas, olive oil, cheese, sea salt, pepper and vinegar and process until puréed. Adjust the seasonings to taste.

Serves 8

The Tea Grotto has been teaching the local Salt Lake City community about the flavorful depths and delicate intricacies of loose-leaf teas since 1994. They focus on sourcing tea from only fair trade and ethical suppliers around the world. The Tea Grotto serves Polenta Pesto Squares with Genmaicha tea. This green tea, made with roasted brown rice, enhances the taste of the pesto and toasted pine nuts.

PARTY TURNOVERS

Turnovers

8 ounces cream cheese, softened

1 1/2 cups all-purpose flour

1/2 cup (1 stick) butter, softened

1 egg, beaten

For the turnovers, mix the cream cheese, flour and butter in a bowl until smooth. Shape into a ball. Chill, wrapped in plastic wrap, for 1 hour. Divide the dough into equal portions. Roll each portion on a floured surface until 1/8 inch thick. Cut into 3-inch circles. Preheat the oven to 450 degrees. Place 1 teaspoon filling on half of each circle. Brush the edge with the egg. Fold in half to enclose the filling. Crimp the edge with a fork and prick the tops. Bake on an ungreased baking sheet for 12 minutes or until golden brown.

Herb Mushroom Filling

8 ounces fresh mushrooms

1 large onion

3 tablespoons butter

1 teaspoon salt

1/4 teaspoon dried thyme leaves

2 tablespoons all-purpose flour

1/4 cup sour cream

For the mushroom filling, mince the mushrooms and onion. Sauté the mushrooms and onion in the butter in a medium skillet over medium heat for 5 minutes. Stir in the salt, thyme and flour. Add the sour cream and mix well.

Ham Filling

3 ounces olives

4 ounces boiled ham, minced

6 ounces cream cheese with chives, softened

For the ham filling, drain and chop the olives. Combine the ham, cream cheese and olives in a bowl and mix well. Pimento-stuffed olives work best in this recipe.

Crab Meat Filling

4 to 6 ounces crab meat, flaked

1/2 cup mayonnaise

1/2 cup (2 ounces) shredded sharp Cheddar cheese

1 tablespoon minced green onions

For the crab meat filling, combine the crab meat, mayonnaise, cheese and green onions in a bowl and mix well. You may add 1 tablespoon capers to the mixture, if desired.

Makes 50 turnovers

BLACK PEPPER ALMONDS

1 tablespoon black pepper

2 teaspoons salt

1/4 cup (1/2 stick) butter

3/4 cup packed brown sugar

4 teaspoons water

2 2/3 cups raw whole almonds

Photograph on page 42.

Preheat the oven to 350 degrees. Mix the pepper and salt in a small bowl. Melt the butter in a large skillet over medium-low heat. Add the brown sugar and water. Cook until the brown sugar dissolves, stirring constantly. Add the almonds and toss to coat. Cook over medium heat for 5 minutes or until the syrup thickens and the almonds are well coated, stirring occasionally. Sprinkle with one-half of the pepper mixture and mix well. Spread on a baking sheet lined with foil, separating the almonds quickly. Sprinkle with the remaining pepper mixture. Bake for 10 minutes or until golden brown. Remove to a wire rack to cool.

Serves 8 to 10

WHITE PEPPER CASHEWS

1 pound cashews

1 egg white

1 1/2 teaspoons salt

1 1/2 teaspoons white pepper

Preheat the oven to 350 degrees. Place the cashews in a bowl. Whisk the egg white in a small bowl until frothy. Pour over the cashews and toss to completely coat the cashews. Add the salt and white pepper and toss to coat evenly. Spread on a baking sheet sprayed with nonstick cooking spray. Bake for 30 to 35 minutes or until toasted. Remove from the oven to cool.

Note: Any kind of nut may be used in this recipe.

Serves 8

Sweet-and-Spicy Nuts

1   pound your favorite nuts,
     such as almonds, cashews,
     peanuts or pecans
1   egg white
1 1/2 teaspoons salt
1   tablespoon brown sugar
1   teaspoon cayenne pepper

Preheat the oven to 350 degrees. Place the nuts in a bowl. Whisk the egg white in a small bowl until frothy. Pour over the nuts and toss to completely coat. Mix the salt, brown sugar and cayenne pepper in a bowl. Add to the nut mixture and toss until the nuts are completely covered. Spread on a baking sheet sprayed with nonstick cooking spray. Bake for 30 to 35 minutes or until the nuts are toasted. Remove from the oven to cool.

Serves 8

Camembert Cheese Crisps

4   ounces Camembert cheese,
     rind removed and cheese
     at room temperature
1/2 cup (1 stick) butter, softened
2/3 cup unbleached
     all-purpose flour
2   dashes of cayenne pepper
1/8 teaspoon salt
     Paprika to taste

Process the cheese and butter in a food processor until creamy. Add the flour, cayenne pepper and salt, pulsing until the dough almost forms a ball. Place on a large sheet of plastic wrap and shape into a loose cylinder 2 inches in diameter. Wrap tightly in the plastic wrap. Chill for 30 minutes. Shape the dough into a smooth even cylinder 8 inches long and about 1 1/2 inches in diameter. Rewrap in the plastic wrap. Chill for 8 to 12 hours.

Preheat the oven to 400 degrees. Cut the cylinder into 1/4-inch slices. Arrange 2 inches apart on a baking sheet. Bake for 10 to 12 minutes or until the edges are brown. Cool on a wire rack. Sprinkle with paprika.

Makes about 2 1/2 dozen

BAKED GOAT CHEESE

1   cup sun-dried tomatoes
2   teaspoons fresh rosemary
    Olive oil
1   (8-ounce) log goat cheese
1   small jar roasted
    red peppers

Combine the sun-dried tomatoes and rosemary in a bowl. Add just enough olive oil to cover. Marinate at room temperature for 2 hours.

Preheat the oven to 350 degrees. Place the cheese in the center of an ovenproof serving dish. Arrange the roasted peppers around the cheese. Spoon the sun-dried tomatoes mixture over the cheese. Add enough olive oil to puddle in the dish. Bake for 10 to 12 minutes or until the cheese is soft and warm. Serve with French baguette slices.

Serves 8 to 10

AMARETTO AND BRIE CHEESE

1/2   cup packed brown sugar
1/4   cup amaretto
1   teaspoon vanilla extract
1   wheel Brie cheese

Melt the brown sugar with the amaretto and vanilla in a small saucepan. Pour over the cheese on a serving platter. Serve with crackers.

Serves 8 to 10

HOLIDAY CRANBERRY CHUTNEY WITH BRIE CHEESE

Cranberry Chutney

1 (16-ounce) can whole berry cranberry sauce

3/4 cup chopped dried apricots

3/4 cup chopped peeled tart green apple

1/4 cup granulated sugar

1/4 cup packed brown sugar

1/3 cup apple cider vinegar

1/4 teaspoon ground allspice

1/4 teaspoon ginger

1/4 teaspoon cinnamon

1/4 teaspoon ground cloves

Brie Cheese

1 small wheel Brie cheese

1/2 cup chopped walnuts or pecans (optional)

For the chutney, combine the cranberry sauce, apricots, apple, granulated sugar, brown sugar, vinegar, allspice, ginger, cinnamon and cloves in a medium saucepan and mix well. Cook over medium-low heat for 25 minutes, stirring occasionally.

For the cheese, preheat the oven to 350 degrees. Place the cheese in the center of a shallow ovenproof serving dish. Pour the chutney over the cheese. Bake for 20 to 25 minutes or until the cheese melts. Remove from the oven and top with the walnuts. Serve with crackers, fresh bread and/or gingersnaps.

Serves 8 to 10

Hell's Backbone Grill Goat Cheese Fondue

Black Pepper Crackers

- 2 cups all-purpose flour
- 1 tablespoon sugar
- 3/4 teaspoon salt
- 1/2 teaspoon cracked black pepper
- 2 tablespoons cold unsalted butter
- 2/3 cup milk

Fondue

- 1 1/4 cups local goat cheese (we use cheese from Shepherds Dairy)
- 8 ounces cream cheese, cut into chunks and softened
- 3 tablespoons chardonnay
- 2 tablespoons Bonny Doon vin de glacier muscat, or other sweet white ice wine
- Pinch of nutmeg

For the crackers, preheat the oven to 425 degrees. Mix the flour, sugar, salt and pepper in a medium bowl. Cut in the butter with a pastry blender until crumbly. Add the milk and mix until moistened. Place on a floured surface. Knead and press the dough into a circle. Cut the dough into halves. Let the dough rest for 5 minutes. Press each dough half into a square. Roll each square evenly into a large rectangle 1/8 inch thick. Cut into desired shapes with a pizza cutter and place on an ungreased baking sheet. Pierce with a fork. Bake for 5 minutes. Rotate the baking sheet. Bake for 3 to 5 minutes longer or until crisp and the edges are golden brown.

For the fondue, melt the goat cheese and cream cheese with the wines in a saucepan over low heat, stirring constantly. Add the nutmeg and whisk until smooth. Pour into a fondue pot. Place the pot in the fondue stand and keep warm over a candle. Serve with the crackers, berries, figs and dried fruit.

Serves 12

Located in the heart of the Grand Staircase-Escalante National Monument, Boulder, Utah, was the last town in the nation to receive year-round mail by automobile. Today, it has no stoplight, cell phone service, ATM, grocery store, or medical facilities. However, it has Zagat-rated Hell's Backbone Grill, which despite all odds, has won the acclaim of national and international media. They serve organic, locally produced, regionally and seasonally appropriate cuisine, growing many of their own vegetables organically on the restaurant's six-acre farm.

CRAB MEAT SPREAD

2 (6-ounce) cans crab meat
2 1/2 cups (10 ounces) shredded
　　 sharp Cheddar cheese
6 green onions, chopped
3 garlic cloves, minced
1 cup mayonnaise

Combine the crab meat, cheese, green onions, garlic and mayonnaise in a bowl and mix well. Scoop into a bowl lined with plastic wrap. Chill for 1 hour or longer to enhance the flavors. Unmold onto a serving plate, discarding the plastic wrap. Serve with crackers.

Serves 8 to 10

WHITE BEAN HUMMUS

1 (15-ounce) can white kidney
　　 beans, drained and rinsed
1 garlic clove
　　 Juice of 1/2 lemon
1/4 cup Italian parsley
1 teaspoon salt
1/2 teaspoon pepper
1/3 cup olive oil

Pulse the beans, garlic, lemon juice, parsley, salt and pepper in a food processor until chopped. Add the olive oil in a fine stream, processing constantly until smooth. Adjust the seasonings to taste. Serve with pita chips, crudités or crostini.

Serves 6 to 8

Blue Cheese Chicken Wing Dip

4 medium boneless skinless
  chicken breasts

8 ounces cream cheese,
  softened

1 (12-ounce) bottle hot wing
  sauce or hot pepper sauce

12 to 16 ounces blue
  cheese dressing

Place the chicken in a medium saucepan and add enough water to cover. Bring to a boil. Reduce the heat and simmer for 10 minutes or until cooked through. Cover and remove from the heat. Let stand for 20 minutes. Drain the chicken and let stand until cool enough to handle. Shred the chicken.

Combine the shredded chicken, cream cheese, hot wing sauce and blue cheese dressing in a medium saucepan. Heat over low heat until hot and bubbly, stirring constantly. Spoon into a serving dish. Serve with carrot sticks, celery sticks and large corn chips.

Serves 16

Clam Dip

1 1/2 cups sour cream

1 (6-ounce) can minced
  clams, drained

1/2 tablespoon granulated garlic

1 tablespoon Worcestershire
  sauce, or more to taste
  Freshly ground pepper
  to taste
  Juice of 1/2 lemon

Combine the sour cream, clams, garlic, Worcestershire sauce, pepper and lemon juice in a small bowl and mix well. Adjust the seasonings to taste. Serve with potato chips.

Serves 6 to 8

Greek Layered Dip

1   pound ground lamb
2   teaspoons Greek seasoning
1   teaspoon garlic salt
2   cups hummus
1 1/2   cups sour cream
1/2   cup finely chopped cucumber
1   cup shredded iceberg lettuce
2   tomatoes on the vine, chopped
1/2   cup chopped red onion
1   (3-ounce) can sliced black olives
8   ounces tomato and basil feta cheese, crumbled

Brown the ground lamb with the Greek seasoning and garlic salt in a large skillet, stirring until crumbly. Drain and set aside. Spread the hummus in a shallow 1 1/2-quart serving dish. Layer the ground lamb, sour cream, cucumber, lettuce, tomatoes, onion, olives and cheese over the hummus in the order listed. Serve with pita chips.

Note: Ground beef may be used instead of ground lamb.

Serves 6 to 8

Green Goddess Dip

1   cup mayonnaise
1   cup chopped green onions
1   cup fresh basil
1/4   cup fresh lemon juice
1   tablespoon grated garlic
1   teaspoon anchovy paste
2   teaspoons salt
1   teaspoon freshly ground pepper
3/4   cup sour cream

Process the mayonnaise, green onions, basil, lemon juice, garlic, anchovy paste, salt and pepper in a blender until smooth. Add the sour cream and process until blended. Spoon into a serving bowl. Chill until serving time. Serve with assorted fresh vegetables such as carrots, celery, cherry tomatoes and jicama.

Serves 6 to 8

YOGURT ONION DIP

2 teaspoons olive oil

1/2 yellow onion, minced

2 cups plain Greek yogurt

3/4 teaspoon onion powder

1 teaspoon garlic powder

1 teaspoon balsamic vinegar

1/2 teaspoon salt

1/4 teaspoon pepper

Heat the olive oil in a skillet. Add the onion and sauté for 10 minutes. Cook, covered, for 10 minutes longer or until the onion is very tender. Remove the onion to a bowl. Cool for 10 minutes. Process the onion and yogurt in a food processor until well mixed. Fold in the onion powder, garlic powder, balsamic vinegar, salt and pepper with a rubber spatula. Chill for 2 hours before serving. Serve with fresh vegetables or chips for dipping.

Serves 12

CRANBERRY JALAPEÑO SALSA

1 (12-ounce) package fresh cranberries, or 6 ounces dried cranberries

1/2 cup jalapeño jelly

1 small jalapeño chile, finely chopped

1 shallot, finely chopped

1/2 cup finely chopped cilantro

Cook the cranberries in a small amount of water until soft; drain. Add the jalapeño jelly, jalapeño chile, shallot and cilantro and mix well. Spoon into a serving bowl. Serve with ham, pork, turkey or chicken as a side dish or as a sandwich relish.

Note: This salsa freezes well.

Serves 6 to 8

Mango Salsa

1   large mango, chopped
1   large avocado, chopped
1   tablespoon minced shallot
    Dash of salt
    Juice of 1 lime

Combine the mango, avocado, shallot, salt and lime juice in a small bowl and mix gently. Serve over grilled chicken or salmon, or serve as a side dish.

Serves 6

RealSalt Chips

5   (8-inch) sprouted whole
    wheat tortillas, or
    10 (6-inch) corn tortillas
1/4 cup cold-pressed
    coconut oil
1   teaspoon Redmond
    RealSalt

Preheat the oven to 350 degrees. Cut the tortillas into triangles. Arrange in a single layer on a baking sheet with space between each one. Bake for 12 to 15 minutes or until crispy. Place in a medium bowl. Add the coconut oil and toss to coat. Add the RealSalt and toss to coat. Let stand until dry before serving.

Serves 4 to

Utah-based RealSalt has a simple philosophy: to provide customers with mineral-rich salt in its natural state. Today, many salts are chemically altered, exposed to heat (which reduces trace minerals), or they include additives like dextrose and anticaking agents. RealSalt is different. It is unrefined, has more than 60 natural trace minerals, and is full of authentic flavor.

SMALL PLATES

Shrimp, Spinach and Goat Cheese Pizza 72 • Rustic Prosciutto and Provolone Sandwich 73
Utah's Own Promontory Cheddar Lamb Burger 73 • Pago's Cinnamon Beets with Nut Crunch
and Truffle Honey 75 • Antipasto Pasta Salad 76 • Asian Chicken Pasta Salad 77
Basil Chicken Pasta Salad 78 • Spinach Chicken Pasta Salad 79 • Santa Rosa Salad 80
Curry Chicken Salad 81 • Honey Cilantro Lime Chicken Salad 81 • Cobb Salad Bites 82
Nutty Apricot Goat Cheese Chicken Salad 83 • Couscous Salad 85 • Orzo Salad with
Spinach and Feta 86 • Orzo Wild Rice Salad 86 • Quinoa and Black Bean Salad 87
Quinoa Salad with Grilled Asparagus, Goat Cheese and Black Olive Vinaigrette 88 • Panzanella 89
Cucumber Salad 90 • Potato Salad 90 • Arugula and Fig Salad with Blue Cheese and
Bacon Vinaigrette 91 • Corn, Cherry Tomato, Arugula and Blue Cheese Salad 92
Citrus Salad Toss 93 • Dried Cherry, Apple and Pecan Salad with Maple Dressing 94
Great Scott Salad 95 • Naked Fish Kudamono Salad 96 • Northwest Autumn Salad 97
Sweet and Crunchy Salad 98 • Roasted Jalapeño, Bacon and Potato Soup 99
Potato Kale Soup 100 • Curry Pumpkin Soup 101 • Zucchini Soup 101
Moroccan Carrot and Sweet Potato Soup 103 • Ribollita 104 • Grilled Tomato Soup 105
Turkey and Vegetable Chili 106 • Turkey White Bean Chili 107 • Spicy White Chili 109
Fresh Chicken Soup 110 • Spicy Coconut Soup 111 • Chicken and Wild Rice Soup 112
Tortilla Soup 113 • Tortellini Soup with Sausage 114 • Salmon Chowder 115

SHRIMP, SPINACH AND GOAT CHEESE PIZZA

8   large shrimp, peeled, deveined
and tails removed
Sea salt and pepper to taste

3   garlic cloves, minced

1/4   cup olive oil
Olive oil for coating
and drizzling

1   recipe pizza dough
Cornmeal and/or
all-purpose flour

1/2   tablespoon pizza seasoning

4   cups torn spinach

4   ounces goat cheese, or
to taste

1   tablespoon balsamic vinegar

Place the shrimp in a bowl. Sprinkle with sea salt and pepper. Add the garlic and toss well. Heat 1/4 cup olive oil in a skillet over medium heat for 2 minutes. Add the shrimp. Cook for 5 minutes or just until the shrimp begin to turn pink. Remove from the heat.

Preheat the oven to 425 degrees. Coat a pizza pan or baking sheet generously with olive oil. Place the dough on a lightly floured surface and sprinkle with some cornmeal and/or flour. Roll the dough into the desired shape and size. Place on the prepared pizza pan. Drizzle lightly with olive oil. Sprinkle with the pizza seasoning and sea salt. Layer the spinach over the dough. Dot with the goat cheese and shrimp. Drizzle the vinegar over the top. Bake for 10 to 20 minutes or until the crust is golden brown.

Note: Fresh asparagus may be used instead of the spinach. This pizza may also be grilled. Preheat the grill to 425 degrees. Place the prepared pizza on a greased grill rack. Grill for 10 to 20 minutes or until the crust is golden brown. The crust will be drier.

Serves 2 to 4

Rustic Prosciutto and Provolone Sandwich

1 cup good-quality mayonnaise

1/4 cup steak sauce

1/4 cup spicy brown mustard

1 French baguette or 1 loaf rustic Italian bread

12 ounces prosciutto

8 ounces provolone cheese

2 cups arugula

Mix the mayonnaise, steak sauce and brown mustard in a bowl. Chill, covered, for a few hours or longer before serving. Cut the baguette lengthwise into halves. Cut the prosciutto and cheese into thin slices. Spread the mayonnaise mixture on the cut side of one-half of the baguette. Layer with the prosciutto, cheese and arugula. Replace the remaining baguette half. Cut into four equal portions to serve.

Serves 4

Utah's Own Promontory Cheddar Lamb Burger

1 pound fresh ground lamb

1 teaspoon minced garlic

2 tablespoons red onion purée

1 teaspoon minced thyme

2 tablespoons chopped Italian parsley

1/2 teaspoon salt

1/2 teaspoon freshly ground pepper

1 egg, beaten

4 focaccia rolls, split

1/2 cup (2 ounces) shredded Beehive Cheese Promontory Cheddar

Preheat the grill. Combine the ground lamb, garlic, onion purée, thyme, parsley, salt, pepper and egg in a bowl and mix well. Shape into four patties. Grill on a grill rack over a medium flame for 3 to 4 minutes on each side or until light pink inside. Remove from the heat. Let stand for 5 minutes. Place the patties on the bottom halves of the rolls. Top with the cheese. Add desired condiments such as aïoli, mustard, lettuce and spring onion. Replace the top halves of the rolls.

Serves 4

One of only a few artisan cheese makers in Utah, Beehive Cheese sources only the creamiest and freshest milk to make their award-winning cheeses. With its name derived from the northern Utah location where the two railroad lines famously linked the country, the Promontory Cheddar used in this recipe is buttery, full-bodied, fruity, and sharp all at the same time.

Pago's Cinnamon Beets with Nut Crunch and Truffle Honey

Nut Crunch

1/4	cup granulated sugar
1/2	cup packed brown sugar
1	tablespoon honey
3	tablespoons butter
1/2	cup almonds, pecans or walnuts
3/4	tablespoon chopped dark chocolate
1	tablespoon all-purpose flour

For the nut crunch, preheat the oven to 325 to 350 degrees. Bring the granulated sugar, brown sugar, honey, butter, almonds and chocolate to a boil in a saucepan. Stir in the flour. Spread as thin as possible on a baking sheet lined with baking parchment or a silicone sheet. Bake for 10 to 15 minutes. Remove from the oven to cool. Chop into pieces.

Cinnamon Beets

2	to 6 small red, gold or striped beets, cooked, peeled and cut into quarters
1	teaspoon cinnamon
1	teaspoon vegetable oil
	Salt and pepper to taste
2	tablespoons Greek yogurt
2	tablespoons truffle honey or regular honey

For the beets, toss the beets with the cinnamon, oil, salt and pepper in a bowl until coated. Arrange on a serving plate. Top each with a dollop of the yogurt. Sprinkle with 1 tablespoon of the nut crunch. Drizzle with the honey. Garnish with micro greens or baby greens.

Serves 2

When Pago first arrived on the Salt Lake City dining scene, word quickly spread that the dish to try was the Cinnamon Beets. "Artisan. Local. Farm Fresh." is the motto at Pago, and creating meaningful relationships with local farms and artisan food producers lies at the heart of each seasonal menu they prepare.

Antipasto Pasta Salad

4   quarts (16 cups) water

2   tablespoons salt

1   tablespoon olive oil

16   ounces rotini

2   teaspoons minced garlic

1/2 teaspoon salt

2   teaspoons balsamic vinegar

1   teaspoon Italian seasoning
     or Herbes de Provence

1/2 teaspoon freshly ground
     black pepper

1/4 teaspoon crushed red
     pepper flakes

6   tablespoons extra-virgin
     olive oil

1 1/2 cups cubed provolone cheese

1   cup thinly sliced oil-pack
     sun-dried tomatoes

1   cup thinly sliced salami

1   cup thinly sliced prosciutto

2   tablespoons finely chopped
     Italian parsley

2   tablespoons finely
     chopped basil

Bring the water, 2 tablespoons salt and 1 tablespoon olive oil to a boil in a large saucepan over high heat. Add the pasta. Cook for 9 minutes or until al dente, stirring occasionally to prevent the pasta from sticking together. Drain the pasta and rinse under cold running water until cool.

Mash the garlic and 1/2 teaspoon salt in a large bowl. Whisk in the vinegar, Italian seasoning, black pepper and red pepper flakes until combined. Whisk in 6 tablespoons olive oil gradually. Add the pasta, cheese, sun-dried tomatoes, salami, prosciutto, parsley and basil and toss to mix. Serve immediately or chill, covered, in the refrigerator and bring to room temperature before serving.

Serves 4 to 6

ASIAN CHICKEN PASTA SALAD

Asian Salad Dressing

1/2 cup canola oil

2 1/2 teaspoons sesame oil

1/2 cup sugar

1 teaspoon salt

3 tablespoons soy sauce

2 tablespoons rice vinegar

1 teaspoon minced garlic

Salad

6 ounces package baby spinach leaves

6 ounces bowtie pasta, cooked and drained

2 to 4 tablespoons sesame seeds, toasted

1/2 cup sunflower seeds

1 (8-ounce) can sliced water chestnuts

3 medium chicken breasts seasoned heavily with lemon pepper, cooked and chopped

1 cup bean sprouts

For the dressing, combine the canola oil, sesame oil, sugar, salt, soy sauce, vinegar and garlic in a mixing bowl and mix well with an electric mixer.

For the salad, toss the spinach, pasta, sesame seeds, sunflower seeds, water chestnuts, chicken and bean sprouts together in a large salad bowl. Add the dressing and toss to coat. Serve at room temperature.

Serves 4 to 6

Basil Chicken Pasta Salad

Italian Salad Dressing

2/3	cup olive oil
5	tablespoons red wine vinegar
1/4	cup basil
3	tablespoons grated Parmesan cheese
1	tablespoon oregano
1	teaspoon salt
1/2	teaspoon pepper

Salad

4	cups chopped cooked chicken
8	ounces rotelle pasta, cooked and rinsed
8	ounces feta cheese, crumbled
1	red bell pepper, thinly sliced
1	green bell pepper, thinly sliced
1 1/2	cups broccoli florets
1	cup cherry tomatoes, cut into halves
1/2	cup mayonnaise

For the dressing, process the olive oil, vinegar, basil, cheese oregano, salt and pepper in a blender until blended.

For the salad, combine the chicken, pasta, cheese, bell peppers, broccoli and tomatoes in a large bowl and mix well. Add the salad dressing and toss to coat. Chill, covered, for 8 to 12 hours. Add the mayonnaise just before serving and toss to coat.

Serves 6 to 8

Spinach Chicken Pasta Salad

Sesame Seed Salad Dressing

1/4	cup sesame seeds
1/3	cup red wine vinegar
1/3	cup soy sauce
3/4	cup vegetable oil
1/3	cup sugar
1/4	teaspoon salt
1/4	teaspoon pepper
1/4	cup chopped green onions
1/4	cup toasted almonds

Salad

4	chicken breasts, poached
16	ounces bowtie pasta, cooked and drained
6	ounces fresh spinach
1	bunch green onions, chopped
2	(11-ounce) cans mandarin oranges, drained
1	(3-ounce) package sugared almonds

For the dressing, process the sesame seeds, vinegar, soy sauce, oil, sugar, salt, pepper, green onions and almonds in a blender until smooth.

For the salad, chop the chicken into 1/2-inch pieces. Combine the chicken and pasta in a large bowl and mix well. Add the dressing and toss to coat. Chill, covered, for 8 to 12 hours. Add the spinach, green onions and mandarin oranges just before serving and toss well. Top with the sugared almonds.

Serves 6 to 8

SANTA ROSA SALAD

Dijon Mustard Salad Dressing

2	garlic cloves, minced
1	tablespoon Dijon mustard
1/2	teaspoon salt
1/4	teaspoon sugar
1/4	teaspoon pepper
1/3	cup rice wine vinegar
1/3	cup olive oil

Salad

1	(8-ounce) package long grain and wild rice
3	large chicken breasts, cooked and chopped
4	green onions, chopped
1	red bell pepper, chopped
3	ounces pea pods, trimmed and blanched
	Juice of 1 large lemon
2	avocados, chopped
1	cup pecans, toasted and chopped

For the dressing, combine the garlic, Dijon mustard, salt, sugar, pepper, vinegar and olive oil in a jar with a tight-fitting lid. Seal the jar with the lid and shake well. Chill in the refrigerator.

For the salad, cook the long grain and wild rice using the package directions. Combine with the chicken, green onions, bell pepper, pea pods and lemon juice in a large bowl and mix well. Add the salad dressing and toss to coat. Chill, covered, for 2 to 4 hours before serving. Top with the avocados and pecans just before serving.

Serves 6

Curry Chicken Salad

1   bunch green onions

1   rib celery

3   pounds boneless skinless chicken breasts, cooked

1   cup dried cranberries

1   cup golden raisins

1   cup sliced almonds

2   cups mayonnaise

1/2 cup rice wine vinegar

2   tablespoons curry powder

1/4 cup apricot preserves

2   tablespoons sugar

2   teaspoons salt

1   teaspoon pepper

1   head radicchio

Cut the green onions and celery diagonally into thin slices. Combine with the chicken, cranberries, raisins and almonds in a large bowl and mix well. Whisk the mayonnaise, vinegar, curry powder, apricot preserves, sugar, salt and pepper together in a small bowl. Add to the chicken mixture and toss to coat. Adjust the seasonings to taste. Serve in radicchio leaves and garnish with edible fresh flowers or snipped herbs.

Serves 8 to 10

Honey Cilantro Lime Chicken Salad

2   to 3 tablespoons minced fresh cilantro

1/4 cup fresh lime juice

2   teaspoons red pepper flakes

2   teaspoons honey

3   boneless skinless chicken breasts, cooked and shredded

1/2 cup canned black beans

1   avocado

10 small grape tomatoes

1/2 cup fresh corn kernels

    Salt and pepper to taste

    Boston lettuce leaves

Whisk the cilantro, lime juice, red pepper flakes and honey together in a large bowl. Add the chicken and toss to coat. Drain and rinse the black beans. Chop the avocado and cut the tomatoes into quarters. Add the corn, black beans, avocado and tomatoes to the chicken and toss gently. Sprinkle with salt and pepper. Serve in the lettuce leaves.

Serves 4

Great for entertaining or any gathering, this dish can be enjoyed traditionally atop a bed of lettuce or used as filling for Mexican-inspired lettuce wraps. For a twist, skip the lettuce and serve with tortilla chips or rice.

COBB SALAD BITES

Blue Cheese Salad Dressing

6	ounces crumbled blue cheese
1	cup mayonnaise
1	cup milk or half-and-half
2	tablespoons red wine vinegar
1	teaspoon salt
1	teaspoon pepper

Salad Bites

2	bunches romaine hearts
1 1/2	cups chopped cooked chicken breasts
1	cup cherry tomatoes, chopped
1	avocado, chopped
2	hard-cooked eggs, finely chopped
1	bunch fresh chives, finely chopped
2	ounces crumbled blue cheese
6	slices bacon, cooked and crumbled

For the salad dressing, process the blue cheese, mayonnaise, milk, vinegar, salt and pepper in a blender until mixed, adding additional milk if needed for the desired consistency. The dressing should be chunky and thick.

For the salad bites, separate the lettuce into leaves. Rinse and pat dry. Arrange the lettuce leaves individually on a serving platter. Dollop the ends of each leaf with the salad dressing. Add a spoonful of the chicken, tomatoes and avocado. Sprinkle each with the chopped eggs, chives, blue cheese and bacon.

Serves 4 to 6

NUTTY APRICOT GOAT CHEESE CHICKEN SALAD

Apricot Salad Dressing

2	tablespoons apricot preserves
1 1/2	tablespoons red wine vinegar
1	teaspoon Dijon mustard
1/4	teaspoon salt
1/4	teaspoon cracked pepper
1/4	cup olive oil

For the salad dressing, mix the apricot preserves, vinegar, Dijon mustard, salt and pepper in a small bowl. Whisk in the olive oil for 30 seconds.

Salad

1	to 2 pounds chicken breasts
	Salt and pepper to taste
2	tablespoons olive oil
1	English cucumber
1/2	small red onion
20	ounces mixed salad greens
14	ounces grape tomatoes, cut into halves
1/4	cup slivered almonds
1/4	cup black walnut pieces
1/4	cup candied cashews
18	ounces fresh raspberries
16	ounces crumbled goat cheese

For the salad, cut the chicken crosswise into slices and pound thin. Sprinkle with salt and pepper. Heat the olive oil in a skillet over medium-high heat. Add the chicken and sauté for 3 minutes on each side or until light golden brown and cooked through. Cut into thin strips. Cut the cucumber into slices and then into halves. Cut the onion into thin slices and then into thin strips. Toss the cucumber, onion, salad greens, tomatoes, almonds, walnut pieces, cashews, raspberries and goat cheese together in a large salad bowl. Add the salad dressing and toss to coat. Add the chicken and toss well. Serve immediately.

Serves 8 to 10

Couscous Salad

1/4 cup extra-virgin olive oil

2 tablespoons fresh lemon juice

2 garlic cloves, minced

1/2 teaspoon grated lemon zest

1 1/3 cups Israeli pearl couscous

Salt to taste

1 3/4 cups (or more) vegetable
broth

8 ounces slender asparagus
spears, cut diagonally into
3/4-inch pieces

8 ounces sugar snap peas,
trimmed and cut into
1/2-inch pieces

8 ounces frozen green
peas, thawed

8 ounces broccolini, cut into
1/2-inch pieces

Pepper to taste

1 pound shrimp, cooked, peeled
and deveined

1/3 cup chopped chives

1/2 cup (2 ounces) grated
Parmesan cheese

Whisk 2 tablespoons of the olive oil, the lemon juice, one-half of the garlic and the lemon zest in a small bowl and set aside.

Heat 1 tablespoon of the remaining olive oil in a heavy medium saucepan over medium heat. Add the couscous and salt. Sauté for 5 minutes or until most of the couscous is golden brown. Add the broth. Increase the heat and bring to a boil. Reduce the heat to medium-low. Simmer, covered, for 10 minutes or until the liquid is absorbed and the couscous is tender, adding additional broth if the couscous is too dry.

Heat the remaining 1 tablespoon olive oil in a heavy large nonstick skillet over high heat. Add the asparagus, sugar snap peas, green peas, broccolini and the remaining garlic. Sprinkle with salt and pepper. Sauté for 3 minutes or until the vegetables are tender-crisp.

Toss the shrimp, sautéed vegetables and couscous together in a large bowl. Drizzle with the dressing. Add the chives and cheese and toss to coat. Sprinkle with salt and pepper.

Serves 6 to 8

Orzo Salad with Spinach and Feta

1/2 cup balsamic vinegar

2 garlic cloves, finely chopped

1/2 teaspoon pepper

1/2 cup olive oil

16 ounces orzo, cooked
and cooled

1/4 cup chopped kalamata
olives, or to taste

1/2 cup chopped red onion

1/2 cup chopped celery

2 green onions, thinly sliced

8 ounces spinach,
coarsely chopped

1/2 cup pine nuts, toasted

6 ounces crumbled feta cheese

Whisk the vinegar, garlic and pepper together in a bowl. Add the olive oil and whisk until the mixture begins to thicken. Combine the pasta, olives, red onion, celery, green onions, spinach, pine nuts and cheese in a large bowl and toss to mix. Add the vinaigrette and toss to coat. Chill for 1 hour before serving.

Note: To toast the pine nuts, preheat the oven to 350 degrees. Place the pine nuts on a baking sheet and bake until golden brown. Or, you may place in a nonstick sauté pan and sauté over medium heat until golden brown, being careful not to burn.

Serves 6 to 8

Orzo Wild Rice Salad

1 cup orzo

1 cup wild rice

1/2 red onion, chopped

4 green onions, sliced

2 ribs celery, coarsely chopped

1 tablespoon parsley

3/4 cup dried cranberries

3/4 cup sliced dried apricots

Zest and juice of
1 large orange

1/4 cup olive oil

Cook the pasta and wild rice separately using the package directions. Let stand until cool. Combine the pasta, wild rice, red onion, green onions, celery, parsley, cranberries, apricots, orange zest, orange juice and olive oil in a large bowl and toss to mix well. Chill, covered, for 1 hour before serving.

Serves 6 to 8

QUINOA AND BLACK BEAN SALAD

Cumin-Lime Dressing

5	tablespoons fresh lime juice
1	teaspoon salt
1 1/4	teaspoons cumin
1/3	cup olive oil

For the dressing, whisk the lime juice, salt and cumin together in a small bowl. Add the olive oil in a fine stream, whisking constantly.

Salad

1 1/2	cups quinoa
3	cups water
1 1/2	cups cooked black beans, rinsed
1 1/2	tablespoons red wine vinegar
	Salt and pepper to taste
1 1/2	cups cooked fresh corn kernels
3/4	cup minced green bell pepper or a mixture of red, yellow and green bell pepper
1	jalapeño chile, seeded and minced
1/4	cup fresh cilantro to taste

For the salad, bring the quinoa and water to a boil in a saucepan. Reduce the heat. Simmer for 15 minutes. Cover and turn off the heat. Let stand for 5 minutes. Fluff with a fork. Place in a large bowl and let stand until cool.

Combine the beans, vinegar, salt and pepper in a small bowl and toss to coat. Add to the quinoa with the corn, bell pepper, jalapeño chile and cilantro and toss to mix. Drizzle with the dressing and toss well. Season with salt and pepper.

Note: The salad may be prepared 1 day ahead and stored, covered, in the refrigerator. Bring to room temperature before serving.

Serves 8 to 10

QUINOA SALAD WITH GRILLED ASPARAGUS, GOAT CHEESE AND BLACK OLIVE VINAIGRETTE

Black Olive Vinaigrette

1/4	cup sherry vinegar
1	tablespoon Dijon mustard
1/2	cup niçoise olives, pitted
1/2	cup olive oil

For the vinaigrette, process the vinegar, Dijon mustard, olives and olive oil in a blender until smooth. Store in the refrigerator.

Salad

12	stalks asparagus, trimmed
	Olive oil for brushing
	Salt and pepper to taste
2	cups red or white quinoa
4	cups water, chicken broth or vegetable broth
2	tablespoons red wine vinegar
2	tablespoons olive oil
1/4	cup Italian parsley, chopped
	Juice of 1/2 lemon
1/2	cup niçoise olives, pitted
1/2	(12-ounce) can black olives
1	cup cherry tomatoes, cut into halves
8	ounces goat cheese

For the salad, preheat the grill. Brush the asparagus with olive oil and sprinkle with salt and pepper. Place on a grill rack. Grill on each side for 2 minutes or just until cooked through. Remove from the grill and cut into halves. Bring the quinoa and water to a boil in a 3-quart saucepan. Reduce the heat. Simmer, covered, for 15 minutes or until all of the water is absorbed and the quinoa appears soft and translucent. Remove from the heat. Let cool for 1 hour. Combine the cooled quinoa, vinegar, 2 tablespoons olive oil, the parsley, lemon juice and 1/4 cup of the Black Olive Vinaigrette in a medium bowl and mix well. Add additional Black Olive Vinaigrette to taste. Add the asparagus, niçoise olives, black olives and tomatoes and mix gently. Place in a serving bowl. Dollop the goat cheese by 1/2 tablespoonfuls on top.

Serves 6 to 8

Panzanella

2/3 cup olive oil

1/4 cup red wine vinegar

1/4 cup lightly packed basil
leaves, chopped

2 tablespoons capers, drained

1/2 teaspoon salt

1/4 teaspoon pepper

1 garlic clove, minced

4 tomatoes

2 cucumbers

1 large yellow bell pepper

1 red onion

1 (12-ounce) loaf Italian bread

1/2 cup kalamata olives

Whisk the olive oil, vinegar, basil, capers, salt, pepper and garlic together in a large bowl. Cut the tomatoes, cucumbers, bell pepper and onion into bite-size pieces and place in a large bowl. Add the vinaigrette and toss to coat. Cut the bread into 1-inch pieces. Add to the vegetables and toss gently to coat. Top with the olives. Garnish with basil leaves.

Serves 12

CUCUMBER SALAD

1/2 cup white vinegar
1 garlic clove, minced
1 teaspoon salt
1/2 teaspoon black pepper
1 teaspoon sugar
   Pinch of red pepper flakes
1 tablespoon minced red bell
   pepper (optional)
1 small red onion, thinly sliced
2 cucumbers, thinly sliced

Combine the vinegar, garlic, salt, black pepper, sugar, red pepper flakes and bell pepper in a medium bowl and stir until the sugar is dissolved. Add the onion and cucumbers and mix well. Chill for at least 1 hour before serving.

Serves 6

POTATO SALAD

8 small red potatoes
2/3 cup mayonnaise
2 tablespoons Dijon mustard
3 or 4 medium
   hard-cooked eggs
4 radishes, sliced
2 to 3 tablespoons chopped
   mixed fresh herbs
2 tablespoons capers

Steam the potatoes in a steamer basket in a saucepan until tender. Let cool completely. Mix the mayonnaise and Dijon mustard in a bowl. Cut the potatoes and eggs into slices $1/8$ inch thick. Arrange on a serving platter. Drizzle with the mayonnaise mixture. Top with the radishes, herbs and capers.

Serves 4

ARUGULA AND FIG SALAD WITH BLUE CHEESE AND BACON VINAIGRETTE

Bacon Vinaigrette

2	slices smoked bacon, cut into thin slices
1/2	large shallot, minced
4	teaspoons balsamic vinegar
1	tablespoon olive oil
1	teaspoon Dijon mustard
	Salt and pepper to taste

Salad

10	fresh figs
1	bunch arugula
1	bunch frisée
4	ounces Saga or Stilton blue cheese

For the vinaigrette, sauté the bacon in a skillet over medium heat until crisp. Drain the bacon, reserving the bacon drippings. Return 1 tablespoon of the reserved drippings to the skillet. Add the shallot and sauté until tender and caramelized. Reduce the heat to low. Whisk in the vinegar, olive oil, Dijon mustard and 2 to 3 tablespoons of the remaining reserved bacon drippings. Cook until heated through. Season with salt and pepper.

For the salad, cut the figs into halves or quarters. Rinse the arugula leaves and frisée well and pat dry. Toss the arugula, frisée, bacon, figs and cheese together in a salad bowl. Drizzle with the vinaigrette.

Note: The salad may be arranged on individual salad plates or on a large platter.

Serves 4

Corn, Cherry Tomato, Arugula and Blue Cheese Salad

2 3/4 cups fresh corn kernels or
frozen corn kernels, thawed
and drained

1 pint cherry tomatoes,
cut into halves

4 ribs celery, chopped

1/2 red onion, chopped

1 1/2 ounces arugula, stems
trimmed and leaves chopped

2 tablespoons balsamic vinegar

1/3 cup olive oil

Salt and pepper to taste

1 cup crumbled blue cheese

Combine the corn, tomatoes, celery, onion and arugula in a large bowl and toss to mix. Pour the vinegar into a small bowl. Whisk in the olive oil gradually. Add salt and pepper. Stir in 3/4 cup of the cheese. Pour over the salad and toss to coat. Sprinkle with the remaining 1/4 cup cheese.

Serves 6 to 8

CITRUS SALAD TOSS

Sugared Pecans

1/4	cup sugar
2/3	cup pecan halves

For the sugared pecans, mix the sugar with the pecans in a small skillet. Cook over low heat until the sugar melts, stirring to coat the pecans well. Spread on a foil-lined surface to cool. Break the pecans apart.

Citrus Salad Dressing

2/3	cup vegetable oil
1/4	cup lime juice
2	tablespoons orange juice
2	tablespoons sugar
1	teaspoon grated lime zest
1	teaspoon grated orange zest

For the salad dressing, combine the oil, lime juice, orange juice, sugar, lime zest and orange zest in an airtight jar and shake well. Chill until serving time.

Salad

8	cups torn leaf lettuce
8	cups torn romaine
1	red onion, thinly sliced
1	large orange, peeled and sliced
1	pint strawberries, cut into halves
2	avocados, thinly sliced

For the salad, toss the leaf lettuce, romaine, onion, orange and strawberries together gently in a large salad bowl. Chill until serving time. Add the avocados just before serving. Drizzle with the salad dressing and toss gently. Top with the sugared pecans.

Serves 4 to 6

DRIED CHERRY, APPLE AND PECAN SALAD WITH MAPLE DRESSING

Maple Dressing

1/4	cup mayonnaise
1/4	cup pure maple syrup
3	tablespoons Champagne vinegar or white wine vinegar
2	teaspoons sugar
1/2	cup vegetable oil
1/8	teaspoon crushed red pepper flakes
	Salt and black pepper to taste

For the dressing, whisk the mayonnaise, maple syrup, vinegar and sugar in a medium bowl until blended. Whisk in the oil gradually until the mixture thickens slightly. Add the red pepper flakes, salt and black pepper. Store in the refrigerator for up to 3 days.

Salad

10	cups lightly packed salad greens
2	Granny Smith apples, cut into matchstick-size strips
1/2	cup dried tart cherries, coarsely chopped
1/2	cup pecans, toasted and chopped
1/2	cup (2 ounces) grated Gruyère cheese

For the salad, toss the salad greens, apples, dried cherries and 1/4 cup of the pecans together in a large salad bowl. Add enough of the salad dressing to coat. Sprinkle with the remaining 1/4 cup pecans and the cheese.

Serves 6 to 8

Great Scott Salad

Mustard Vinaigrette

1	cup red wine vinegar
3/4	cup sugar
1	small red onion, chopped
2	teaspoons dry mustard
1	teaspoon salt
1/2	cup vegetable oil

For the salad dressing, process the vinegar, sugar, onion, dry mustard and salt in a blender until blended. Add the oil in a fine stream, processing constantly.

Salad

8	ounces almonds, sliced
3	tablespoons sugar
2	apples
1	large head iceberg lettuce, torn into pieces
1	large head green leaf lettuce, torn into pieces
1	large head red leaf lettuce, torn into pieces
8	ounces mushrooms, sliced
1	pound bacon, cooked and crumbled
8	ounces mozzarella cheese, shredded
8	ounces Parmesan cheese, grated
1/2	cup dried cranberries or raisins

For the salad, cook the almonds with the sugar in a small skillet over medium heat until the sugar caramelizes and the almonds are golden brown, stirring constantly. Remove to waxed paper to cool. Cut the apples into bite-size pieces. Toss the iceberg lettuce, green leaf lettuce, red leaf lettuce, mushrooms, bacon, mozzarella cheese, Parmesan cheese, dried cranberries, almonds and apples together in a large salad bowl. Add the dressing just before serving and toss to coat.

Serves 8 to 10

Naked Fish Kudamono Salad

Spice Mixture

1	tablespoon minced garlic
1	teaspoon chopped fresh parsley
1	tablespoon onion powder
1	tablespoon dried oregano
1	teaspoon dried thyme
1/4	teaspoon celery salt
4	teaspoons black sesame seeds

For the spice mixture, mix the garlic, parsley, onion powder, oregano, thyme, celery salt and sesame seeds in a small bowl. Store, covered, in the refrigerator.

Kudamono Salad Dressing

1/2	onion, grated
1	tablespoon Dijon mustard
1/3	cup rice vinegar
1/3	cup fresh orange juice
1/2	cup sugar
1	cup extra-virgin olive oil

For the salad dressing, process the onion, Dijon mustard, vinegar, orange juice and sugar in a blender until blended. Add the olive oil gradually, processing constantly. Add 2 tablespoons of the spice mixture and blend well. Reserve the remaining spice mixture for another purpose.

Salad

4	cups mixed salad greens, rinsed and spun dry
4	ounces blueberries
8	strawberries
1	Asian pear, cut into 1-inch pieces
1	cup (1-inch) pineapple pieces
1	cup (1-inch) papaya pieces
2	ounces caramelized pecans
2	ounces fresh soft goat cheese, such as Shepherd's feta cheese

For the salad, toss the salad greens with the salad dressing in a large salad bowl to coat. Add the blueberries, strawberries, pear, pineapple and papaya and toss well. Top with the pecans and cheese.

Serves 4

———

The Naked Fish's Kudamono Salad (kudamono means "fruit" in Japanese) is prepared with fruits, cheeses, and greens that vary depending on what is in season and can be locally sourced. Take their cue and experiment with combinations of seasonal fruits and local cheeses.

———

Northwest Autumn Salad

Lemon-Maple Vinaigrette

1/2	cup vegetable oil
1/4	cup cider vinegar
2	tablespoons minced shallots
2	tablespoons lemon juice
1	tablespoon maple syrup
1/4	teaspoon salt
1/4	teaspoon pepper

Salad

2	Pink Lady apples
1	head red leaf lettuce, torn into bite-size pieces
1	head Bibb lettuce, torn into bite-size pieces
1	cup watercress leaves
3/4	cup glazed pecans or walnuts
3/4	cup crumbled blue cheese

For the vinaigrette, combine the oil, vinegar, shallots, lemon juice, maple syrup, salt and pepper in an airtight container and shake well.

For the salad, cut the apples into thin wedges. Toss the red leaf lettuce, Bibb lettuce, watercress, apples, pecans and cheese together in a large salad bowl. Add the salad dressing and toss to coat. Serve immediately.

Serves 4 to 6

SWEET AND CRUNCHY SALAD

Red Wine Vinaigrette

- 1/2 cup olive oil
- 6 tablespoons sugar or sugar substitute
- 1/4 cup red wine vinegar
- 3 tablespoons minced red onion
- 1/2 teaspoon salt
- 1/2 teaspoon dry mustard

For the vinaigrette, combine the olive oil, sugar, vinegar, onion, salt and dry mustard in an airtight container and shake to mix well. Chill in the refrigerator. Bring to room temperature before serving and shake to mix well.

Salad

- 2 or 3 heads mixed salad greens, rinsed, torn and spun dry
- 6 to 8 scallions, chopped
- 1 small red bell pepper, chopped
- 2 carrots, shredded
- 1/2 cup honey-roasted peanuts, chopped
- 4 ounces blue cheese, crumbled
- 1/2 red onion, thinly sliced
- 2 cups chow mein noodles

For the salad, toss the salad greens, scallions, bell pepper, carrots, peanuts and cheese together in a large salad bowl. Add the vinaigrette just before serving and toss to coat. Top with the onion slices. Add the chow mein noodles and toss to coat.

Serves 8 to 10

ROASTED JALAPEÑO, BACON AND POTATO SOUP

8 ounces smoked bacon, chopped (about 8 slices)
1 1/2 cups chopped onions
1 cup chopped celery
3/4 cup chopped red bell pepper or yellow bell pepper
3 garlic cloves, minced
1/4 teaspoon dried thyme
1 teaspoon salt
1/8 teaspoon freshly ground black pepper
Pinch of cayenne pepper
1 tablespoon finely chopped roasted jalapeño chiles, or to taste
6 cups chicken stock
3 cups chopped red potatoes
1/2 cup (1 stick) butter
1/4 cup all-purpose flour
1 cup (4 ounces) shredded Cheddar cheese
2 cups (about) cream or half-and-half
White wine vinegar to taste

Cook the bacon in a large saucepan over low heat until crisp. Remove the bacon with a slotted spoon to paper towels to drain, reserving the drippings in the saucepan. Add the onions, celery and bell pepper to the reserved drippings. Cook for 10 minutes or until the onions are translucent. Add the garlic and thyme. Cook for 1 minute, stirring constantly. Add the salt, black pepper, cayenne pepper, jalapeño chiles, stock and potatoes. Bring to a boil. Reduce the heat and simmer for 15 minutes or until the potatoes are cooked through.

Melt the butter in a small saucepan. Stir in the flour. Cook over medium heat, stirring constantly. Do not brown. Stir into the potato mixture to blend. Simmer for 3 minutes or until the soup thickens, stirring constantly. Add the cheese. Cook until melted, stirring constantly. Stir in enough of the cream to reach the desired consistency. Add a splash of vinegar. Reserve some of the bacon for serving time. Stir the remaining bacon into the soup. Ladle into soup bowls. Sprinkle with the reserved bacon.

Serves 6

POTATO KALE SOUP

1   bunch kale

2   pounds potatoes

1   onion, chopped

4   garlic cloves, chopped

2   teaspoons olive oil

2   quarts (8 cups) chicken
    stock or vegetable stock

1   tablespoon stone-ground
    mustard

1/2   cup dry white wine

1   teaspoon salt
    Pepper to taste

1/4   cup heavy cream (optional)

Rinse the kale and chop the leaves and stems. Scrub and chop the potatoes. Sauté the onion and garlic in the olive oil in a large saucepan until the onion is translucent. Add the potatoes and stock. Bring to a boil. Reduce the heat and simmer for 15 minutes or until the potatoes are soft. Add the kale, mustard, wine, salt and pepper. Simmer, covered, for 10 minutes or until the kale is tender. Purée a portion of the soup in a food processor or blender and return to the saucepan, if desired. Stir in the cream. Ladle into soup bowls. Garnish with freshly cracked pepper.

Serves 6

CURRY PUMPKIN SOUP

2   tablespoons unsalted butter
1   cup chopped onion
2   garlic cloves, minced
1 1/2   teaspoons curry powder
1   teaspoon garam masala
    Salt and pepper to taste
3   cups chicken stock or
    vegetable stock
1   (15-ounce) can pumpkin
1   (12-ounce) can
    evaporated milk

Melt the butter in a large saucepan. Add the onion and garlic. Sauté for 2 to 3 minutes or until tender, stirring frequently. Stir in the curry powder, garam masala, salt and pepper. Cook for 1 minute. Add the stock and pumpkin and bring to a boil. Reduce the heat to low. Simmer for 15 to 20 minutes, stirring occasionally. Stir in the evaporated milk. Process in batches in a food processor until smooth. Ladle into soup bowls.

Serves 6 to 8

ZUCCHINI SOUP

6   to 8 slices bacon, chopped
1   onion, chopped
1   garlic clove, minced
6   to 8 zucchini, cut into
    1/2-inch slices
2   (10-ounce) cans chicken broth
2   cups water
1   teaspoon salt
1/8   teaspoon pepper
1   tablespoon basil
1/4   cup chopped fresh parsley
    Grated Parmesan cheese
    Croutons

Cook the bacon in a large saucepan until crisp. Drain, reserving 1 tablespoon of the bacon drippings with the bacon. Add the onion and garlic to the reserved drippings and bacon. Sauté until the vegetables are tender. Add the zucchini, broth, water, salt, pepper, basil and parsley. Bring to a boil. Reduce the heat and simmer for 15 minutes. Purée 2 cups at a time in a blender. Ladle into soup bowls. Sprinkle with cheese and croutons.

Serves 8

Moroccan Carrot and Sweet Potato Soup

2 tablespoons unsalted butter

1 teaspoon fennel seeds

2 pounds carrots, peeled
and sliced

1 pound sweet potatoes,
peeled and chopped

2 large Granny Smith apples,
peeled and chopped

1 large sweet onion, chopped

6 cups vegetable broth

2 tablespoons long grain rice

1/4 teaspoon curry powder

1/4 teaspoon coriander

1/8 teaspoon ground allspice

2 large bay leaves

Salt and pepper to taste

Heat the butter in a large saucepan over medium heat. Add the fennel seeds. Cook for 2 to 3 minutes or until fragrant, stirring frequently. Add the carrots, sweet potatoes, apples and onion. Cook for 5 minutes, stirring frequently. Add the broth, rice, curry powder, coriander, allspice and bay leaves. Bring to a boil. Reduce the heat and simmer for 30 minutes or until the vegetables are tender. Discard the bay leaves. Purée the soup in batches in a food processor or with an immersion blender. Sprinkle with salt and pepper. Ladle into soup bowls.

Serves 6

RIBOLLITA

1/4 cup olive oil

6 slices pancetta or
bacon, chopped

2 carrots, chopped

2 ribs celery, chopped

1 onion, chopped

3 or 4 garlic cloves, minced

2 tablespoons tomato paste

4 cups chicken stock or
vegetable stock
Salt and pepper to taste
Leaves from 1 sprig of thyme

2 potatoes, peeled and
chopped

1/2 head green cabbage, shredded

1 bunch Swiss chard, shredded

1 bunch kale, shredded

4 cups chicken stock or water

1 (15-ounce) can
cannellini beans

6 to 8 slices dry bread
Extra-virgin olive oil
Shaved Parmesan cheese or
Pecorino Romano cheese

Heat 1/4 cup olive oil in a large saucepan over medium heat. Add the pancetta, carrots, celery, onion and garlic. Sauté until soft but not brown. Add the tomato paste. Cook for 2 minutes, stirring constantly. Add 4 cups stock, salt, pepper and thyme. Bring to a boil. Reduce the heat and simmer for 15 minutes. Add the potatoes, cabbage, chard and kale. Add 2 cups of the stock or water. Return to a boil. Reduce the heat and simmer for 45 minutes, adding the remaining 2 cups stock or water to maintain a soup thick enough for a spoon to almost stand up. Add the beans. Cook for 5 minutes. Adjust the seasonings to taste.

Remove the soup from the heat. Add the bread by pulling back the soup with a wooden spoon and sliding each slice underneath. Let stand to cool. Reheat the soup over medium heat until bubbly. Ladle into huge soup bowls. Drizzle with extra-virgin olive oil and sprinkle with cheese.

Note: You may use 1 small can tomato sauce, or 2 or 3 chopped tomatoes instead of the tomato paste.

Serves 6

GRILLED TOMATO SOUP

4 pounds Roma tomatoes and grape tomatoes

1/4 cup olive oil

4 garlic cloves, minced

Salt and pepper to taste

2 tablespoons olive oil

1 large yellow onion

1 fennel bulb

1/2 cup red wine

4 cups chicken broth

3 tablespoons tomato paste

1 tablespoon balsamic vinegar

2 cups packed fresh basil leaves

1 teaspoon fresh thyme leaves

Preheat the grill. Combine the tomatoes, 1/4 cup olive oil, one-half of the garlic, salt and pepper in a bowl and toss to coat. Place in a grill basket. Grill over medium heat for 10 to 15 minutes or until the tomatoes are splitting open and slightly blackened, stirring occasionally.

Heat 2 tablespoons olive oil in a Dutch oven. Add the remaining garlic, the onion and fennel. Cook until the vegetables are tender. Add the grilled tomatoes, wine, broth and tomato paste. Bring to a boil. Reduce the heat and simmer for 30 to 45 minutes. Add the vinegar, basil, thyme, salt and pepper. Remove from the heat. Blend with an immersion blender until the soup is of the desired consistency. Ladle into soup bowls. Garnish with chopped fresh basil and Parmesan cheese.

Note: The tomatoes may be roasted instead of grilled. To roast, preheat the oven to 400 degrees. Place the tomato mixture in a single layer on a large baking sheet lined with foil. Roast for 45 minutes.

Serves 8

TURKEY AND VEGETABLE CHILI

1 1/2 pounds ground turkey
1 tablespoon canola oil
2 cups chopped onions
2/3 cup chopped carrots
2 garlic cloves, minced
4 cups water
2 cups frozen corn kernels
1 cup chopped red bell pepper
1 cup chopped zucchini
3 tablespoons chili powder
2 teaspoons dried oregano
2 tablespoons ground cumin
1/4 teaspoon salt
2 (28-ounce) cans crushed
   tomatoes
2 (16-ounce) cans pinto beans,
   drained and rinsed
2 (16-ounce) cans kidney beans,
   drained and rinsed
2 (15-ounce) cans black beans,
   drained and rinsed
1 (6-ounce) can tomato paste
1 1/2 tablespoons rice vinegar
1 1/2 teaspoons finely chopped
   canned chipotle chile in
   adobo sauce

Brown the ground turkey in a skillet, stirring until crumbly. Heat the oil in a large stockpot over medium-high heat. Add the onions, carrots and garlic. Sauté for 5 minutes. Stir in the water, corn, bell pepper, zucchini, chili powder, oregano, cumin, salt, tomatoes, beans and tomato paste. Stir in the ground turkey. Bring to a boil. Cover and reduce the heat. Simmer for 25 minutes or until the carrots are tender, stirring occasionally. Stir in the vinegar and chipotle chile. Ladle into soup bowls.

Note: Shredded cheese and sour cream may be stirred into the chili for added flavor.

Serves 16

TURKEY WHITE BEAN CHILI

1   can chipotle chiles
1/2 cup water
1   pound tomatillos
1   large onion, chopped
4   garlic cloves, minced
2   tablespoons vegetable oil
1   tablespoon ground cumin
1   pound ground turkey
1   cup chicken broth
1   bay leaf
1   teaspoon salt
3/4 teaspoon oregano
1   large bell pepper, chopped
1   (4-ounce) can chopped
    green chiles
2   (16-ounce) cans white beans,
    drained and rinsed
1   tablespoon cornmeal
1/4 cup cilantro, chopped

Process the chipotle chiles with the water in a food processor until blended. Remove the husks from the tomatillos. Blanch the tomatillos in water to cover in a saucepan; drain. Purée the tomatillos in a food processor. Cook the onion and garlic in the oil in a stockpot until the onion is soft. Add the cumin. Cook for 30 seconds. Add the ground turkey and cook until no longer pink, stirring until crumbly. Add the chipotle chiles, tomatillos, broth, bay leaf, salt and oregano. Simmer for 1 hour. Stir in the bell pepper, green chiles, beans and cornmeal. Simmer for 30 minutes. Discard the bay leaf. Stir in the cilantro just before serving. Ladle into soup bowls.

Serves 4 to 6

Spicy White Chili

1 large chicken breast
2 jalapeño chiles
2 to 3 tablespoons olive oil
1 yellow onion, chopped
1 garlic clove, minced
1 tablespoon all-purpose flour
2¹/2 cups chicken stock
1 (16-ounce) can white
   beans, drained
1 (16-ounce) can
   cannellini beans
¹/2 teaspoon ground cumin
¹/2 teaspoon chili powder
¹/2 teaspoon salt
1 teaspoon freshly
   ground pepper
1 bay leaf
   Kernels from 2 large ears
   of white sweet corn
6 tablespoons sour cream
3 to 4 tablespoons
   chopped cilantro
1 large avocado, sliced

Boil the chicken in water to cover in a saucepan until cooked through. Remove from the heat to cool. Shred the chicken, discarding the skin and bones.

Chop the jalapeño chiles, removing the seeds from one of the chiles. Heat the olive oil in a saucepan over medium heat. Add the jalapeño chiles, onion and garlic. Sauté until the onion is translucent. Stir in the flour to coat the vegetables. Add 1 cup of the stock and bring to a boil. Add 1 cup of the remaining stock, the beans, cumin, chili powder, salt, pepper and bay leaf. Bring to a boil. Add the corn, chicken and remaining ¹/2 cup stock. Bring to a boil. Reduce the heat and simmer for 20 minutes. Discard the bay leaf. Ladle into serving bowls. Dollop each serving with 2 tablespoons sour cream, 1 heaping tablespoon cilantro and the avocado.

Serves 3

FRESH CHICKEN SOUP

1 cup chopped onion
1 cup chopped carrots
2 garlic cloves, minced
6 cups vegetable broth
1/4 cup white rice
1 teaspoon ground cumin
1 (16-ounce) can Great
   Northern beans, drained
   and rinsed
3 cups chopped cooked chicken
1/2 cup chopped fresh cilantro
1/2 teaspoon pepper
1/4 teaspoon salt
1 tablespoon fresh lime juice

Heat a stockpot over medium-high heat and coat with nonstick cooking spray. Combine the onion, carrots and garlic in the prepared stockpot. Sauté for 3 minutes. Add the broth, rice, cumin and beans. Bring to a boil. Reduce the heat and simmer for 15 minutes. Stir in the chicken, cilantro, pepper and salt. Simmer for 5 minutes or until the chicken is heated through. Remove from the heat. Stir in the lime juice. Ladle into soup bowls.

Note: Leftover cooked rice may be used, but omit simmering for 15 minutes.

Serves 6

This crowd pleaser can be personalized by each guest with lime wedges, fresh tomato, avocado, and sour cream. Intensify the flavor with cayenne pepper, hot sauce, or jalapeño chiles. Transform the recipe into an Asian-style soup by omitting the beans and substituting 1 teaspoon grated fresh ginger for the cumin. Garnish with mung bean sprouts and chopped green onions.

SPICY COCONUT SOUP

1 or 2 galangal

1 serrano chile

White portion of 4 or
5 stalks lemon grass, bruised

1 to 2 tablespoons vegetable oil

1 teaspoon chopped
fresh ginger

1 to 2 tablespoons chopped
green onions

1 1/2 (14-ounce) cans unsweetened
coconut milk

1 quart (4 cups) chicken stock
Zest from 2 limes

1/4 to 1/2 teaspoon green curry
paste, or to taste

1/4 to 1/2 teaspoon curry powder
(optional)

1 tablespoon light brown sugar

1/4 to 1/3 cup cilantro, chopped

3 tablespoons Asian fish sauce

1 to 2 pounds assorted
mushrooms (shiitake, cremini,
oyster, straw), chopped

1/4 cup fresh lime juice

6 to 8 ounces snow peas,
trimmed and julienned

1/4 cup basil, chopped

1/2 boneless chicken breast,
cut into 1/2×2-inch strips

Peel the galangal and cut into thin discs. Seed and mince the serrano chile. Coarsley chop the lemon grass.

Heat the oil in a saucepan. Add the galangal, ginger, serrano chile, lemon grass and green onions and sauté for 2 minutes. Do not brown. Add the coconut milk, stock, lime zest, curry paste, curry powder, brown sugar, cilantro and fish sauce. Simmer for 10 to 15 minutes to infuse the flavors. Strain into a Dutch oven, discarding the solids. Add the mushrooms. Simmer for 20 to 30 minutes. Add the lime juice, snow peas, basil and chicken. Simmer for 5 to 10 minutes or until the chicken is cooked through. Ladle into soup bowls.

Note: This soup is as good or better served the next day. You may use homemade chicken stock in this recipe if you have it on hand. Galangal is a spicy root with a gingery, pepper flavor that is popular in Thai cooking. You can find it in most Asian markets.

Serves 4 to 6

CHICKEN AND WILD RICE SOUP

1   yellow onion, chopped

2   tablespoons vegetable oil

2   cups julienned carrots

1   cup white wine

1/2 cup (1 stick) unsalted butter

3/4 cup all-purpose flour

4   to 5 cups milk

4   large boneless skinless
    chicken breasts, cooked and
    chopped or shredded

2   cups wild rice mix, cooked

2   to 3 tablespoons dried parsley
    Salt and pepper to taste

2   to 4 (14-ounce) cans
    chicken broth

Sauté the onion in the oil in a large stockpot until tender. Add the carrots and wine. Simmer until the carrots are tender.

Melt the butter in a saucepan. Add the flour gradually, stirring until smooth. Whisk in the milk. Cook until the sauce is thick and bubbly, stirring constantly. Add the chicken, rice and white sauce to the vegetables in the stockpot and mix well. Stir in the parsley, salt, pepper and broth. Cook until heated through. Ladle into soup bowls.

Note: Poultry seasoning and oregano may be added, if desired.

Serves 6 to 8

TORTILLA SOUP

2 tablespoons olive oil
4 small corn tortillas,
   cut into pieces
1 large onion, chopped
2 tablespoons jalapeño chiles,
   seeded and minced
5 garlic cloves, minced
2 tablespoons tomato paste
4 (15-ounce) cans
   whole tomatoes
1 tablespoon ground cumin
4 (14-ounce) cans chicken broth
2 cups chopped cooked chicken
   Salt and pepper to taste
1 cup chopped avocado
1/2 cup (2 ounces) shredded
   sharp Cheddar cheese
1/2 cup chopped fresh cilantro

Heat the olive oil in a large Dutch oven. Add the tortillas. Cook for 2 minutes or until soft. Add the onion, jalapeño chiles and garlic and sauté for 3 minutes. Add the tomato paste and undrained tomatoes. Bring to a simmer. Cook for 10 minutes. Add the cumin, broth and chicken. Bring to a boil. Reduce the heat to medium and simmer for 30 minutes. Add salt and pepper. Process with an immersion blender until smooth. Ladle into soup bowls. Top with the avocado, cheese and cilantro.

Note: Instead of using an immersion blender, process the soup in three batches in a food processor or blender until smooth.

Serves 12

TORTELLINI SOUP WITH SAUSAGE

1 pound maple pork sausage
1 small onion, chopped
1 (28-ounce) can crushed
   tomatoes
3 (14-ounce) cans
   chicken broth
2 cups apple juice
1 cup water
1 teaspoon basil
1 teaspoon oregano
   Salt and pepper to taste
   Frozen vegetables or fresh
   vegetables to taste
1 (20-ounce) package fresh
   cheese tortellini

Brown the sausage in a stockpot, stirring until crumbly; drain. Add the onion and cook until tender. Add the tomatoes, broth, apple juice, water, basil, oregano, salt and pepper. Simmer for 30 minutes or longer. Add frozen vegetables and the tortellini. Cook for 5 to 10 minutes or until heated through. Ladle into soup bowls.

Note: If using fresh vegetables, cook with the sausage.

Serves 6 to 8

SALMON CHOWDER

1/2 cup finely chopped onion
1/2 cup finely chopped celery
1/4 cup finely chopped green
     bell pepper
1   garlic clove, finely chopped
1   (14-ounce) can
     chicken broth
2   cups diced peeled
     Yukon Gold potatoes
1   cup diced carrots
1   teaspoon seasoned salt
1/2 teaspoon dill weed
1   (14-ounce) can
     cream-style corn
1   (12-ounce) can
     evaporated milk
2   cups chopped cooked salmon

Cook the onion, celery, bell pepper and garlic in one-fourth of the broth in a large saucepan until tender. Add the remaining broth, potatoes, carrots, seasoned salt and dill weed. Simmer, covered, for 20 minutes or until the vegetables are tender. Add the corn, evaporated milk and salmon. Cook until heated through. Ladle into soup bowls. Garnish with fresh dill weed, cream and a pat of butter.

Note: Fresh zucchini may be added after the other vegetables are tender and simmered for 5 minutes.

Serves 7

LARGE PLATES

Baked Stuffed Flank Steak 118 • Barbecued Brisket 119 • Grilled Tri-Tip Roast 120
Company Stroganoff 121 • Mongolian Beef with Bean Sprouts 123 • Roasted Garlic Beef Stew 124
Beef and Fresh Vegetable Marinara Sauce 125 • Tamale Pie 126 • Papa Rellena 127
Eggplant Parmesan Burger 128 • Veal Marsala 129 • Asian Pork Tenderloin 130 • Porketta 130
Apple-Stuffed Pork Chops 131 • Crab-Stuffed Pork Chops 132 • Provençal Spareribs with
Roasted Potatoes and Brussels Sprouts 133 • Best Barbecued Spareribs 134 • Mexican Pork 134
Pork Ragù 135 • Fresh Corn Polenta with Sausage, Chard and Oyster Mushrooms 136
Eggplant and Sausage Pasta 137 • Pressed Italian Sandwich 139 • Fresh Barbecued Chicken 140
Honey Walnut Chicken 141 • Cranberry Chicken 142 • Indian Chicken 142 • Chicken Saltimbocca
with Country Ham 143 • Yakitori 144 • Chicken Fingers 144 • Chicken Potpie 145
Chicken Shish Kabobs 146 • Chicken Pasta with Ham and Sun-Dried Tomatoes 147 • Pesto Chicken
with Penne 147 • Pasta with Chicken and Sun-Dried Tomatoes 148 • Chicken Stir-Fry
Lettuce Cups 148 • Thai Chicken in Spicy Peanut Sauce 149 • Cilantro Lime Chicken Fajitas 150
Sweet Potato Chicken Curry 151 • Turkey Vegetable Meatloaf 151 • Herb Salt-Rubbed Rack of Lamb
with Honey-Vinegar Reduction 153 • Marguerite Henderson's Coffee and Spice Lamb Kabobs with
Lemon Mint Rice 154 • Spiced Morgan Valley Lamb Shoulder Chops 155 • Tapenade Lamb Kabobs
and Couscous 156 • Goldener Hirsch Inn's Duck Confit with Riesling Choucroute 157
Log Haven Quinoa-Crusted Crab Cakes 158 • Meditrina's Curry Lime Prawns 159
Tiger Prawns with Tomatoes and Pasta 160 • Shrimp with Lemon Herb Butter Sauce 160
Garlic and Ginger Shrimp with Rice Noodles 161 • Foil-Baked Halibut 162
Squatters' Captain Bastard's Stout Salmon 162 • Cedar-Planked Salmon with Chef's Dressing 163
Pacific Salmon with Roasted Red Pepper Beurre Pomme 164 • Fish Tacos 165 • Citrus Fish 166
Tilapia in a Parmesan Cheese Sauce 166 • Black Bean and Goat Cheese Enchiladas 167
Stir-Fried Bok Choy and Shiitake Mushrooms 168 • Vegetarian Tikka Masala 169
Orecchiette with Fresh Mozzarella Cheese 169

Baked Stuffed Flank Steak

Rice Stuffing

1/2	cup (1 stick) butter, softened
1 1/2	cups cooked rice
1/2	cup chopped onion
1/2	cup chopped parsley
1	garlic clove, crushed
1/2	cup (2 ounces) grated Parmesan cheese
1/2	teaspoon salt
1/2	teaspoon pepper

For the stuffing, mix the butter, rice, onion, parsley, garlic, cheese, salt and pepper in a bowl and mix well.

Flank Steak

1	(2-pound) flank steak
2	garlic cloves, crushed
1	tablespoon soy sauce
1/4	teaspoon pepper
2	tablespoons butter
1/2	cup condensed beef broth
1/2	cup water (optional)
1	tablespoon chopped crystallized ginger, or
	3/4 teaspoon ground ginger

For the steak, preheat the oven to 350 degrees. Wipe the steak with a damp paper towel. Score both sides lightly into diamond shapes with a sharp knife. Rub both sides with the garlic. Brush with the soy sauce and sprinkle with the pepper. Spread 1 tablespoon of the butter over one side of the steak. Arrange the stuffing over the steak to within 1 1/2 inches from each edge. Roll up to enclose the stuffing; secure with skewers. Spread the remaining 1 tablespoon butter over the top. Place in a roasting pan. Dilute the broth with the water and pour over the steak. Sprinkle with the ginger. Roast for 45 to 60 minutes or to the desired degree of doneness, basting occasionally with the pan juices. Serve with the pan juices.

Serves 4

Barbecued Brisket

Barbecue Sauce

- 1/2 cup (1 stick) butter
- 3/4 cup ketchup
- 1/2 cup packed brown sugar
- 3 tablespoons lemon juice
- 1 tablespoon Dijon mustard
- 2 teaspoons A.1. steak sauce
- 2 teaspoons Tabasco sauce, or to taste
- 2 teaspoons Worcestershire sauce

For the barbecue sauce, bring the butter, ketchup, brown sugar, lemon juice, Dijon mustard, steak sauce, Tabasco sauce and Worcestershire sauce to a boil in a saucepan, stirring frequently. Reduce the heat and simmer to the desired consistency.

Brisket

- 1 large brisket
- 1 envelope dry onion soup mix
- 1 (12-ounce) can beer

For the brisket, preheat the oven to 275 degrees. Place the brisket in a 9×13-inch baking pan lined with foil. Sprinkle with the soup mix. Pour the beer over the top. Bake, covered with foil, for 4 to 6 hours or until tender. Shred the brisket and place in a serving bowl. Add the barbecue sauce and mix well. Serve warm with cocktail-size buns.

Note: The barbecue sauce may be doubled.

Serves 8

GRILLED TRI-TIP ROAST

7   garlic cloves, chopped

1/3 cup olive oil

4   teaspoons salt

1   teaspoon black peppercorns

1   (2- to 2 1/2-pound) tri-tip
    roast, with a thin layer of fat

Process the garlic, olive oil, salt and peppercorns in a blender to form a coarse paste. Pat the roast dry with a paper towel. Score the fat layer with a sharp knife, cutting through the fat layer but not the meat. Place in a sealable plastic bag and add the garlic paste. Press the air from the bag and seal. Massage the bag to coat the roast with the garlic paste. Marinate at room temperature for 1 hour or longer, refrigerating if marinating for more than 2 hours and bringing to room temperature before grilling.

Place 4 ounces of oak or hickory chips in a bowl and cover with water. Place an inverted plate on top to keep the chips submerged. Ignite about fifty charcoal briquettes in a chimney on the grill. Preheat until the flames subside and the coals are covered with white ash. Dump the coals from the chimney into a mound on one side of the grill. Drain the wood chips and scatter across the hot coals. Place the roast fat side down on the grill rack. Sear directly over the flame for 3 to 4 minutes on each side, turning once. Move the roast to the cool side of the grill and replace the lid with the vents open. Grill for 20 to 25 minutes for medium-rare, or for 25 to 30 minutes for medium or to the desired degree of doneness, checking the temperature of the roast every 4 or 5 minutes. Remove to a serving platter. Let stand for 10 minutes for the juices to settle. Cut diagonally across the grain into 1/4-inch slices. Spoon the carving juices over the roast and serve.

Serves 4 to 6

COMPANY STROGANOFF

All-purpose flour

Salt and pepper to taste

2 pounds sirloin steak,
 cut into strips

4 tablespoons (or more)
 butter

1 onion, chopped

8 ounces mushroom caps

4 ounces mushrooms, sliced

3 garlic cloves, chopped

4 cups (about) dry vermouth

2 cups sour cream

12 ounces egg noodles, cooked
 and drained

Place flour, salt, pepper and the steak in a sealable plastic bag and shake to coat. Melt 2 tablespoons of the butter in a large heavy skillet until sizzling. Shake off the excess flour from the steak and add the steak to the hot butter. Add the onion. Cook until the steak is brown, adding additional butter if needed. Sauté the mushrooms in the remaining 2 tablespoons butter in a skillet until nearly tender. Add the garlic and sauté until the mushrooms are tender, adding additional butter if needed. Spoon over the steak. Add 2 cups of the vermouth. Simmer for several hours or until tender, adding the remaining vermouth as needed. Stir in the sour cream just before serving and cook until heated through. Serve over the hot noodles.

Serves 4 to 6

MONGOLIAN BEEF WITH BEAN SPROUTS

1 tablespoon grated fresh ginger

1 garlic clove, minced

1 teaspoon sesame oil

3 tablespoons brown sugar

1/4 cup soy sauce

1 teaspoon cornstarch

Dash of red pepper flakes

1 1/2 pounds beef fillet,
cut into strips

2 tablespoons vegetable oil

8 ounces fresh bean sprouts

1 pound snow peas, trimmed

Dash of salt

Dash of sugar

Hot cooked rice (optional)

Combine the ginger, garlic, sesame oil, brown sugar, soy sauce cornstarch and red pepper flakes in a bowl and mix well. Add the beef and toss to coat. Marinate at room temperature for 30 minutes, turning occasionally.

Preheat a wok over high heat. Spoon 1 tablespoon of the vegetable oil into the hot wok. Add the beef. Stir-fry for 3 to 4 minutes or until the beef is cooked through, stirring to scrape up any brown bits. Remove to a platter or large bowl. Spoon the remaining 1 tablespoon vegetable oil into the wok. Add the bean sprouts and snow peas. Stir-fry for 1 minute. Sprinkle with the salt and sugar. Add to the beef and toss to mix. Serve immediately over hot rice.

Serves 4 to 6

Roasted Garlic Beef Stew

12 garlic cloves

1 tablespoon butter, melted

1 pound stew beef

1 tablespoon all-purpose flour
  Salt and pepper to taste

3 tablespoons butter

4 large potatoes, peeled
  and chopped

2 to 4 large carrots, cut into
  1/2-inch slices

2 (14-ounce) cans beef broth

1 broth can dry red wine

1 tablespoon dried thyme,
  crumbled

2 teaspoons dried rubbed sage

1 tablespoon butter, softened

1 tablespoon all-purpose flour

Preheat the oven to 350 degrees. Toss the unpeeled garlic in 1 tablespoon melted butter in a bowl. Place on a small baking sheet. Bake for 15 minutes. Remove from the oven and cool for 5 minutes. Peel the garlic. Toss the beef with 1 tablespoon flour, salt and pepper in a bowl. Melt 3 tablespoons butter in a large stockpot over high heat. Add the beef. Sauté for 6 minutes or until light brown. Add the potatoes, carrots, broth, wine, thyme, sage and roasted garlic. Bring to a simmer. Simmer for 30 minutes or until the vegetables are tender. Mix 1 tablespoon butter with 1 tablespoon flour in a bowl. Stir into the stew. Cook until thickened, stirring constantly. Sprinkle with salt and pepper.

Note: The stew may be cooked in a slow cooker on High for 4 hours or on Low for 6 to 8 hours.

Serves 4

BEEF AND FRESH VEGETABLE MARINARA SAUCE

4 garlic cloves

2 white onions

1 large red bell pepper

1 large yellow bell pepper

2 large carrots

2 large ribs celery

10 ounces baby bella
mushrooms

1/2 cup olive oil

1/2 teaspoon salt

1/2 teaspoon black pepper

10 grinds of garlic and black
pepper seasoning

33/4 pounds fresh vine-ripened
tomatoes, puréed

2 large bay leaves

1/2 teaspoon crushed red
pepper flakes

1 teaspoon sugar

1/4 teaspoon oregano

1 teaspoon Tony Chachere's
original Creole seasoning

11/2 pounds 96/4 lean ground beef

Chop the garlic, onions, bell peppers, carrots, celery and mushrooms. Heat the olive oil in a 5-quart saucepan over medium-high heat. Add the garlic and onions and sauté for 10 minutes or until the onions are translucent. Add the bell peppers, carrots, celery, mushrooms, salt, black pepper and garlic and black pepper seasoning. Sauté for 10 minutes or until all of the vegetables are soft. Add the tomatoes, bay leaves, red pepper flakes, sugar, oregano and 1/2 teaspoon of the Creole seasoning. Simmer over low heat.

Sprinkle the remaining 1/2 teaspoon Creole seasoning over the beef. Brown the beef in a 10-inch nonstick skillet over medium heat, stirring until crumbly; drain. Stir into the sauce mixture. Simmer over low heat for 1 hour or until thickened, stirring frequently. Discard the bay leaves before serving.

Note: The recipe may be prepared 1 day ahead. Cool and chill, covered, until ready to serve. Reheat over medium heat. Canned crushed tomatoes may be used instead of the fresh tomatoes.

Serves 15

TAMALE PIE

1 pound ground beef or
  ground turkey
1 green bell pepper, chopped
2 garlic cloves, minced
2 teaspoons chili powder
1 teaspoon ground cumin
1/2 teaspoon salt
1 (10-ounce) can mild
  enchilada sauce
1 (15-ounce) can kidney
  beans, drained and rinsed
1 cup frozen or canned
  corn kernels
1 cup (4 ounces) shredded
  Cheddar cheese
1 (8-ounce) package corn
  bread mix
1/3 cup milk
1 egg

Preheat the oven to 400 degrees. Brown the ground beef with the bell pepper in a large deep nonstick skillet over medium-high heat, stirring until crumbly; drain. Stir in the garlic, chili powder, cumin and salt. Add the enchilada sauce, beans and corn. Bring to a simmer over medium heat. Simmer for 5 minutes. The mixture will be thick. Spread in an 8- or 9-inch baking dish. Top with the cheese. Mix the corn bread mix, milk and egg in a bowl just until moistened. Spread evenly over the cheese layer. Bake for 18 to 20 minutes or until golden brown. Let stand for 5 minutes before serving.

Serves 6

Papa Rellena

6 large Yukon gold potatoes
1 egg
 Salt and pepper to taste
12 ounces ground beef
1 1/2 onions, chopped
2 garlic cloves, minced
1 tablespoon vegetable oil
1 large tomato, chopped
1 teaspoon chopped parsley
1/2 cup white wine
1 hard-cooked egg, chopped
 All-purpose flour
 Vegetable oil for frying

Boil the potatoes in water to cover in a saucepan until tender; drain. Mash the potatoes. Add the egg, salt and pepper. Brown the ground beef with the onions and garlic in 1 tablespoon oil in a skillet, stirring until the ground beef is crumbly. Add the tomato, parsley, wine, hard-cooked egg, salt and pepper. Cook until the mixture thickens, stirring frequently. Shape the mashed potato mixture into balls and fill with the ground beef mixture. Roll in flour to coat. Fry in hot oil in a skillet until brown.

Serves 6 to 8

Eggplant Parmesan Burger

1 pound 85/15 ground chuck

1/2 cup bread crumbs

1 egg

1 tablespoon finely chopped fresh rosemary

1 tablespoon finely chopped fresh oregano

1 eggplant

Salt to taste

2 ciabatta

Olive oil

Garlic powder to taste

1 (6-ounce) package sun-dried tomatoes

11/4 cups (5 ounces) freshly grated Parmesan cheese blend

Mix the ground chuck, bread crumbs, egg, rosemary and oregano together in a bowl. Divide the mixture into four equal portions. Shape each portion into a patty.

Peel the eggplant and cut into thick slices. Sprinkle with salt. Place in a single layer on a microwave-safe platter. Microwave on High for 3 minutes or until tender.

Cut the bread into four burger-size buns. Cut each bun into halves horizontally. Brush the cut sides of each bun half with olive oil.

Preheat the grill. Place the beef patties on a grill rack. Sprinkle liberally with salt and garlic powder. Grill until the juices begin to form on top of the patties and then turn. Place the eggplant slices on the grill rack. Grill for 3 minutes. Place enough eggplant slices on each patty to cover. Place the sun-dried tomatoes on top of the eggplant and sprinkle liberally with the cheese. Place the buns oiled side down on the grill rack. Grill until toasted and golden brown. Continue to grill, covered, until the patties are cooked through and the cheese is melted. Place the patties on one-half of the bread slices. Top with the remaining bread slices and serve. For added punch, try adding whole fresh basil leaves.

Serves 4

Veal Marsala

8   (4-ounce) veal cutlets
3/4 teaspoon salt
3/4 teaspoon pepper
1/4 cup (1/2 stick) unsalted butter
2   tablespoons olive oil
1   large shallot
4   garlic cloves
10   ounces assorted mushrooms,
     sliced (baby bella, cremini,
     oyster, shiitake)
1/2 teaspoon salt
1/4 teaspoon pepper
1/2 cup sweet marsala
2   sprigs of fresh rosemary
3/4 cup chicken broth
1   (10-ounce) can cream of
     mushroom soup
     Salt and pepper to taste

Sprinkle the veal with 3/4 teaspoon salt and 3/4 teaspoon pepper. Melt 1 tablespoon of the butter and 1 tablespoon of the olive oil in a large heavy skillet over medium-high heat. Add one-half of the veal. Cook for 1 1/2 to 2 minutes on each side or until golden brown. Remove with tongs to a platter. Repeat with the remaining veal, adding 1 tablespoon of the remaining butter and the remaining 1 tablespoon olive oil to the skillet. Set the veal aside.

Melt 1 tablespoon of the remaining butter in the pan drippings. Add the shallot and garlic and sauté for 30 seconds. Add the mushrooms, 1/2 teaspoon salt and 1/4 teaspoon pepper. Sauté for 3 minutes or until the mushrooms are tender. Add the wine and rosemary sprigs. Simmer for 2 minutes. Add the broth and soup. Simmer for 4 to 5 minutes, stirring frequently. Return the veal to the skillet, turning to coat with the sauce. Cook for 2 minutes. Stir in the remaining 1 tablespoon butter. Season with salt and pepper to taste. Discard the rosemary sprigs. Place the veal on individual serving plates and top with the sauce.

Serves 4

ASIAN PORK TENDERLOIN

1	(1-inch) piece fresh ginger, minced
1	jalapeño chile, seeded and minced
1/4	teaspoon red pepper flakes
1/3	cup honey
3	tablespoons soy sauce
3	tablespoons sesame oil
23/4	pounds pork tenderloin

Mix the ginger, jalapeño chile, red pepper flakes, honey, soy sauce and sesame oil together in a bowl. Pour over the pork in a sealable plastic bag and seal tightly. Marinate in the refrigerator for 1 to 4 hours.

Preheat the grill. Drain the pork, reserving the marinade. Place the pork on a grill rack. Grill to 145 degrees on a meat thermometer. Let stand for 5 minutes. Boil the reserved marinade in a saucepan until thickened, stirring frequently.

To serve, cut the pork diagonally into 1/2-inch slices and top with the sauce. Serve with roasted carrots and garlic mashed potatoes.

Serves 4

PORKETTA

1	(4-pound) pork butt roast
1	tablespoon salt
11/2	teaspoons crushed black pepper
4	teaspoons fennel seeds
1	tablespoon olive oil
2	tablespoons chopped garlic

Preheat the oven to 350 degrees. Cut small slits in the pork. Mix the salt, pepper and fennel seeds together. Mix the olive oil and garlic together in a bowl. Pour over the cuts in the pork. Spread the fennel seed mixture over the pork. Roast for 11/2 to 2 hours or until tender and cooked through. Shred the pork and serve with buttered hard rolls.

Serves 6 to 8

APPLE-STUFFED PORK CHOPS

1 (6-ounce) package stuffing mix
  for pork or chicken
1/2 cup chopped peeled apple
1/4 cup sweetened dried
  cranberries
4 (1 1/4-inch-thick) boneless
  center-cut pork chops
1/2 teaspoon salt
1/4 teaspoon pepper

Preheat the oven to 425 degrees. Prepare the stuffing mix using the package directions. Stir in the apple and dried cranberries. Cut a pocket in the side of each pork chop with a sharp knife. Place on a foil-lined baking sheet. Sprinkle with the salt and pepper. Stuff each pork chop with 1/2 cup of the stuffing and press to flatten. Arrange any remaining stuffing around the pork chops. Bake for 18 to 20 minutes or until the pork chops are cooked through. Preheat the broiler. Broil for 2 to 3 minutes or until the pork chops are brown on top.

Serves 4

CRAB-STUFFED PORK CHOPS

 1   (6-ounce) can lump
     crab meat, drained
1/4 cup bread crumbs
 1   egg
 1   tablespoon anchovy paste
1/2 teaspoon sesame oil
1/2 teaspoon salt
 1   rib celery, finely chopped
1/2 onion, chopped
 5   mushrooms, minced
 4   pork loin chops, butterflied

Preheat the oven to 350 degrees. Combine the crab meat, bread crumbs, egg, anchovy paste, sesame oil and salt in a bowl and mix well. Sauté the celery, onion and mushrooms in a skillet until the mushrooms lose all of their moisture Add to the crab meat mixture and mix well. Divide into four equal portions Spread each portion on one side of each pork chop. Fold the other side of the pork chop over the stuffing. Place on a lightly greased baking sheet. Bake for 30 to 35 minutes or until the stuffing reaches 160 degrees on a meat thermometer.

Serves 4

PROVENÇAL SPARERIBS WITH ROASTED POTATOES AND BRUSSELS SPROUTS

4 pounds pork spareribs

2 tablespoons extra-virgin olive oil

3 or 4 dashes of coarse sea salt

5 garlic cloves, coarsely chopped

1/2 teaspoon fennel seeds

2 tablespoons coarsely chopped fresh rosemary leaves

1 1/4 cups flat-leaf parsley, coarsely chopped

3 or 4 sprigs of fresh thyme

1 pound small potatoes

1 pound Brussels sprouts

2 or 3 garlic cloves, slivered

Coarse sea salt to taste

2 tablespoons extra-virgin olive oil

Cut the spareribs into two-rib portions. Toss the spareribs with 2 tablespoons olive oil, 3 or 4 dashes of sea salt, the chopped garlic, fennel seeds, rosemary, parsley and thyme in a large bowl to coat. Marinate, covered, in the refrigerator for 1 to 12 hours.

Preheat the oven to 350 degrees. Arrange the spareribs in a single layer in a large roasting pan with the curved meatier side down. Spoon any of the remaining marinade over the top. Roast for 1 hour.

Scrub the potatoes and cut into halves. Parboil in water to cover in a saucepan for 6 minutes; drain. Trim the Brussels sprouts of any rough outer leaves. Cut into pieces and slices, using any loose leaves. Turn the spareribs over and place in the center of the pan. Arrange the potatoes and Brussels sprouts in a single layer around the spareribs. Sprinkle with the slivered garlic and sea salt to taste. Drizzle 2 tablespoons olive oil over the vegetables. Bake for 30 minutes. Stir the vegetables; drain. Bake for 20 to 30 minutes longer or until the spareribs and vegetables are tender.

Serves 4

BEST BARBECUED SPARERIBS

1   rack of pork spareribs
2   cups water
1   cup ketchup
1/2 cup packed brown sugar
1/4 cup vinegar
1/4 cup Worcestershire sauce
1   teaspoon celery salt
1   teaspoon chili powder

Preheat the oven to 450 degrees. Place the spareribs in a large baking pan. Bake for 20 minutes. Reduce the oven temperature to 250 degrees. Mix the water, ketchup, brown sugar, vinegar, Worcestershire sauce, celery salt and chili powder in a saucepan. Boil for 3 minutes. Drain the spareribs. Pour half the sauce over the spareribs. Bake for 3 hours, turning once. Serve the remaining sauce with the spareribs.

Serves 4

MEXICAN PORK

1   pound dried pinto beans
2   pounds country-style
    pork ribs
2   garlic cloves, minced
2   tablespoons chili powder
1   teaspoon oregano
    Salt to taste
1   tablespoon Tabasco sauce
    or other hot pepper sauce

Sort and rinse the beans. Place the beans, ribs, garlic, chili powder, oregano and salt in a slow cooker. Cover with water. Cook on High for 8 hours. Remove the ribs to a platter. Shred the pork, discarding the bones. Return the pork to the slow cooker and mix well. Add the Tabasco sauce and mix well. Serve over tortilla chips with toppings of shredded lettuce, chopped tomatoes, shredded cheese, chopped onions, sliced black olives, salsa, sour cream, guacamole and/or hot chiles.

Serves 4 to 6

PORK RAGÙ

1 (3¼-pound) boneless
   pork shoulder roast,
   cut into quarters
5 or 6 dashes of kosher salt
5 or 6 dashes of ground pepper
1 cup all-purpose flour
2 tablespoons olive oil
¾ cup chopped pancetta
1 large yellow onion, chopped
3 carrots, peeled and cut into
   ¾-inch pieces
3 fennel bulbs, cut into
   ½-inch slices
1 tablespoon minced garlic
1 tablespoon olive oil
1¾ pounds cremini,
   cut into quarters
1 (28-ounce) can diced
   tomatoes, drained
3 tablespoons mushroom
   demi-glace
3 tablespoons tomato paste
1 cup red wine
1 cup chicken broth
12 ounces pappardelle, cooked
   al dente and drained

Sprinkle the pork with the kosher salt and pepper. Dredge the pork in the flour, shaking off the excess. Heat 2 tablespoons olive oil in a large saucepan. Cook the pork in batches for 8 minutes or until brown on all sides, removing to a platter after each addition. Reduce the heat to medium. Add the pancetta to the drippings in the saucepan. Cook for 3 to 5 minutes or until brown, stirring occasionally. Add the onion, carrots and fennel. Cook for 5 to 6 minutes or until tender. Add the garlic. Cook for 1 minute, stirring constantly. Remove to a bowl using a slotted spoon.

Increase the heat and add 1 tablespoon olive oil to the drippings in the saucepan. Add the mushrooms. Cook for 15 minutes or until brown. Remove to a bowl. Add the tomatoes, demi-glace, tomato paste, wine and broth to the drippings in the saucepan. Bring to a simmer. Add the pork, pancetta mixture and mushrooms and mix well. Place in a heated slow cooker. Cook, covered, on High for 5 hours or until the pork is very tender. Fold in the pasta to coat. Spoon onto serving plates and garnish with chopped flat-leaf parsley.

Serves 8 to 10

Fresh Corn Polenta with Sausage, Chard and Oyster Mushrooms

Polenta

- 2 small ears of fresh corn
- 2 cups chicken broth or vegetable broth
- 1 cup cornmeal
- 1 tablespoon olive oil
- 1 tablespoon chopped spicy red chile, such as serrano, cheyenne, etc.
- 1/2 teaspoon salt
- 1/2 teaspoon pepper

For the polenta, shuck the corn and remove the silks. Cut the corn kernels from the cobs into a bowl. Bring the broth to a boil in a saucepan. Add the cornmeal. Cook over medium heat for 10 to 15 minutes or until the broth is absorbed, stirring occasionally. Add the corn kernels, olive oil, spicy red chile, salt and pepper just before serving. Cook for a few minutes longer if needed to remove any excess moisture.

Topping

- 3 or 4 links Italian sausage, casings removed
- 1 to 2 cups sliced oyster mushrooms
- 2 garlic cloves, minced
- 1 large bunch of Swiss chard, kale or spinach

For the topping, cook the sausage in a medium saucepan until cooked through. Remove to a plate, reserving the drippings in the saucepan. Add the mushrooms and garlic to the reserved drippings and sauté until tender. Add the chard and sauté until wilted, adding additional olive oil if needed. Add the sausage. Spoon the polenta into serving bowls and top with the chard and mushroom mixture.

Serves 4

EGGPLANT AND SAUSAGE PASTA

16 ounces penne

2 pounds bulk hot and spicy
Italian sausage

1 eggplant, peeled and chopped

1 sweet onion or yellow
onion, chopped

2 garlic cloves, minced

2 tablespoons olive oil

1 (28-ounce) can diced
tomatoes

1 (6-ounce) can tomato paste

1 teaspoon salt

1 teaspoon pepper

1 teaspoon dried basil

1 teaspoon paprika

15 ounces whole milk
ricotta cheese

4 cups (16 ounces) shredded
mozzarella cheese

Preheat the oven to 350 degrees. Cook the pasta using the package directions; drain. Brown the sausage in a skillet over medium heat, stirring until crumbly; drain. Sauté the eggplant, onion and garlic in the olive oil in a large skillet until tender. Stir in the tomatoes, tomato paste, salt, pepper, basil and paprika. Simmer, partially covered, for 15 minutes. Remove from the heat. Stir the pasta into the eggplant mixture. Stir in the sausage. Spread one-half of the sausage mixture in a greased 9×13-inch baking dish. Spread with the ricotta cheese. Sprinkle with one-half of the mozzarella cheese. Layer the remaining sausage mixture over the top. Bake, covered, for 40 minutes. Uncover and sprinkle with the remaining mozzarella cheese. Bake for 5 minutes or until the mozzarella cheese melts. Let stand for 10 minutes before serving.

Serves 6

PRESSED ITALIAN SANDWICH

1 1/2 teaspoons Dijon mustard
1 tablespoon balsamic vinegar
1/4 cup olive oil
2 tablespoons warm water
Salt and pepper to taste
1 loaf rustic Italian bread
1/2 cup pesto or black
olive spread
1 (12-ounce) jar oil-pack
roasted red bell peppers
8 ounces goat cheese or
feta cheese
6 ounces prosciutto,
thinly sliced
4 ounces peppered salami,
thinly sliced
4 to 6 slices provolone cheese
1 (8-ounce) jar marinated
artichoke hearts
2 1/4 cups chopped fresh herbs
(basil, cilantro and parsley)

Mix the Dijon mustard and vinegar in a small bowl. Whisk in the olive oil gradually. Whisk in the warm water. Season with salt and pepper. Cut the bread into halves horizontally. Brush the cut sides with some of the vinaigrette and spread with the pesto. Arrange the bell pepper strips on the bottom half of the bread. Crumble the goat cheese over the bell pepper strips. Alternate layers of the prosciutto, salami and provolone cheese over the goat cheese until all of the ingredients are used. Drizzle with some of the remaining vinaigrette. Top with the artichoke hearts. Sprinkle with the herbs. Drizzle with the remaining vinaigrette. Replace the top half of the bread. Wrap the sandwich very tightly with plastic wrap, wrapping lengthwise and around the width. Set a heavy brick, cast-iron skillet or other heavy object on top of the sandwich. Chill in the refrigerator for 1 hour or longer. To serve, unwrap the sandwich and cut into strips or wedges.

Serves 6 to 10

This flavorful and hearty sandwich is as versatile as your pantry. Substitute different meats and cheeses or create an entirely vegetarian option. The sandwich can be made with a rustic Italian loaf or a round "hubcap" loaf. It is ideal for a picnic, tailgate party, or outdoor concert any way it is prepared.

Fresh Barbecued Chicken

Barbecue Sauce

1/4	cup orange juice
1/2	cup mild chili sauce
2	tablespoons molasses
1	tablespoon soy sauce
2	teaspoons whole grain mustard
1	tablespoon white wine vinegar
1	teaspoon Worcestershire sauce
1/2	teaspoon Tabasco sauce
1/2	teaspoon salt

For the sauce, mix the orange juice, chili sauce, molasses, soy sauce, mustard, vinegar, Worcestershire sauce, Tabasco sauce and salt in a small saucepan. Bring to a boil. Reduce the heat and simmer for 5 minutes. Remove from the heat and cool to room temperature.

Chicken

2	teaspoons smoked paprika
2	teaspoons kosher salt
	Zest of 1 large lemon
1/2	teaspoon granulated garlic
1/2	teaspoon freshly ground pepper
4	chicken legs with thighs
2	chicken breasts

For the chicken, mix the paprika, kosher salt, lemon zest, granulated garlic and pepper in a small bowl. Sprinkle evenly over the chicken pieces. Let stand at room temperature for 30 minutes. Preheat the grill. Place the chicken pieces skin side down on a grill rack. Grill, with the lid closed, over direct medium heat for 8 to 10 minutes or until golden brown, turning occasionally. Move the chicken pieces to indirect medium heat. Continue to grill, with the lid closed, for 20 minutes. Brush both sides of the chicken pieces with a thin layer of the sauce. Grill for 15 minutes longer or until the juices run clear and the chicken is no longer pink at the bone, turning occasionally and brushing with some of the remaining sauce. Serve warm or at room temperature with the remaining sauce on the side.

Serves 4

Honey Walnut Chicken

Honey Walnuts

1	cup sugar
1 1/2	tablespoons water
1/2	cup honey
1 1/2	cups walnut halves
1/2	cup peanut oil

Chicken

1	egg white
1/2	teaspoon salt
2	teaspoons cornstarch
1	tablespoon water
4	large boneless skinless chicken breasts, cut into 1/2-inch pieces
2	tablespoons soy sauce
1/4	cup grated fresh ginger
2	garlic cloves, minced
2	tablespoons oyster sauce
2	teaspoons pepper
2	tablespoons rice wine
2	teaspoons sugar
1	tablespoon cornstarch
2	tablespoons water
4	green onions, shredded
	Hot steamed rice

For the walnuts, heat the sugar, water and honey in a saucepan until the sugar and honey are liquefied. Stir in the walnuts and remove from the heat. Let stand for 3 1/2 to 12 hours.

Reheat the walnut mixture until the sugar and honey are liquefied again; drain. Heat the peanut oil to 350 degrees in a wok. Fry the drained walnuts in batches in the hot oil until amber brown. Remove from the oil and set aside.

For the chicken, whip the egg white, salt, 2 teaspoons cornstarch and 1 tablespoon water in a large bowl until foamy. Add the chicken and stir to coat. Chill for 30 minutes or longer.

Combine the soy sauce, ginger, garlic, oyster sauce, pepper, wine and sugar in a bowl and mix well. Add the undrained chicken to the drippings in the wok, stirring constantly to separate the pieces. Add the soy sauce mixture and stir to coat. Whisk 1 tablespoon cornstarch into 2 tablespoons water in a bowl. Add to the chicken mixture and stir-fry until the sauce is thickened and the chicken is cooked through. Stir in the green onions and honey walnuts. Serve over steamed rice.

Serves 4

CRANBERRY CHICKEN

4 boneless chicken breasts
1/2 cup dried cranberries
1/2 cup crumbled feta cheese
1/4 cup lemon juice
1/4 cup olive oil
 Dash of salt
 Dash of pepper
1 tablespoon minced
 fresh parsley

Preheat the oven to 400 degrees. Cut each chicken breast horizontally to but not through to form a pocket. Stuff each with a mixture of the dried cranberries and cheese. Place in a 9×13-inch baking dish. Mix the lemon juice and olive oil in a bowl. Pour over the chicken. Sprinkle with salt and pepper. Bake, covered, for 25 minutes. Increase the oven temperature to 425 degrees. Bake, uncovered, for 5 minutes longer or until crisp on top. Sprinkle with the parsley.

Note: You may substitute the fresh herb of your choice for the parsley.

Serves 4

INDIAN CHICKEN

8 boneless skinless
 chicken breasts
 Juice of 1 lemon
1 1/2 teaspoons salt
2 tablespoons plain yogurt
1 tablespoon vegetable oil
1/2 small red onion
2 garlic cloves, minced
1 small piece of fresh ginger,
 chopped
4 teaspoons tomato paste
2 teaspoons coriander
1 1/2 teaspoons ground cumin
1 1/2 teaspoons paprika
1/2 teaspoon salt

Toss the chicken with the lemon juice and 1 1/2 teaspoons salt in a large bowl. Process the yogurt, oil, onion, garlic, ginger, tomato paste, coriander, cumin, paprika and 1/2 teaspoon salt in a food processor to form a paste. Add to the chicken and toss to coat. Marinate in the refrigerator for 15 to 30 minutes.

Preheat the grill. Place the chicken on a grill rack. Grill for 8 to 10 minutes on each side or to 165 degrees on a meat thermometer. Serve with hot cooked basmati or jasmine rice.

Note: Serve **Cilantro Yogurt Sauce** over the chicken, if desired. Mix 1/2 cup plain yogurt, 2 tablespoons chopped cilantro, 1/4 teaspoon paprika and a pinch of salt together in a bowl.

The chicken may be broiled instead of grilled. Place the chicken on a foil-lined broiler pan. Preheat the broiler. Broil for 5 to 6 minutes on each side or to 165 degrees on a meat thermometer.

Serves 8

CHICKEN SALTIMBOCCA WITH COUNTRY HAM

4   to 6 chicken breasts
16 to 24 fresh sage leaves,
    coarsely chopped
8   to 12 very thin slices
    country ham or prosciutto
1/4 cup all-purpose flour
    Pepper to taste
2   tablespoons olive oil
1/4 cup dry white wine
1/4 cup marsala or port
3/4 cup chicken stock
    Coarse salt to taste

Place each chicken breast between two sheets of plastic wrap and pound 1/4 inch thick. Sprinkle the chicken with the sage. Top each with 1 or 2 slices of ham and press lightly to adhere. Place on a baking sheet. Chill for 10 minutes or longer to set.

Mix the flour and pepper in a shallow dish. Heat the olive oil in a skillet. Dredge two pieces of the chicken in the flour mixture to lightly coat, shaking off the excess. Place ham side down in the hot olive oil. Cook for 2 to 3 minutes on each side, turning once. Remove to a platter and cover loosely with foil. Repeat with the remaining chicken.

Pour off any excess oil from the skillet and return the skillet to the heat. Pour in the white wine and marsala. Bring to a boil over medium heat, stirring to scrape up any brown bits. Add the stock. Increase the heat to high. Cook for 3 to 5 minutes or until the sauce is reduced and slightly thickened, stirring frequently. Sprinkle with coarse salt and pepper to taste. Serve over the chicken.

Serves 4 to 6

Yakitori

1/2 cup low-sodium soy sauce

1/2 cup turbinado sugar

1 strip of lemon zest

4 to 6 boneless skinless
chicken thighs

Preheat the grill to 350 degrees. Heat the soy sauce, turbinado sugar and lemon zest in a saucepan over low heat until the sugar dissolves. Pound the chicken 1/2 inch thick. Dip into the soy sauce mixture and place on a grill rack. Grill for 8 to 10 minutes or until cooked through. Bring the remaining soy sauce mixture to a boil. Boil for 2 to 3 minutes. Drizzle over the chicken. Serve with hot cooked rice sprinkled with seasoned rice vinegar.

Serves 4 to 6

Chicken Fingers

1 1/2 cups sour cream

1/4 cup lemon juice

1 teaspoon paprika

1 teaspoon
Worcestershire sauce

1/2 teaspoon pepper

4 garlic cloves, minced

6 boneless skinless chicken
breasts, cut into strips

1 cup dry Italian bread crumbs

3/4 cup (3 ounces) grated
Parmesan cheese

6 tablespoons butter, melted

1/4 cup chopped fresh parsley

Mix the sour cream, lemon juice, paprika, Worcestershire sauce, pepper and garlic in a one-gallon sealable plastic bag. Add the chicken and seal the bag. Marinate in the refrigerator for 8 to 12 hours. Remove the chicken from the bag and discard the marinade.

Preheat the oven to 325 degrees. Mix the bread crumbs with the cheese in a large bowl. Coat the chicken with the bread crumb mixture. Place in a 9×13-inch baking dish sprayed with nonstick cooking spray. Drizzle with 3 tablespoons of the butter. Bake for 30 minutes. Drizzle the remaining 3 tablespoon butter over the chicken. Bake for 15 minutes or until golden brown. Sprinkle with the parsley.

Serves 6

CHICKEN POTPIE

Celery Seed Pastry

2	cups all-purpose flour
2	teaspoons celery seeds
1	teaspoon salt
2/3	cup shortening, lard or unsalted butter
4	to 5 tablespoons cold water

For the pastry, mix the flour, celery seeds and salt in a medium bowl. Cut in the shortening until crumbly. Sprinkle with the water 1 tablespoon at a time, tossing with a fork until all of the flour is moistened and the dough pulls from the side of the bowl. Shape the dough into a ball.

Potpie

1/3	cup butter
1/3	cup chopped onion
1/3	cup all-purpose flour
1/2	teaspoon salt
1/2	teaspoon dried thyme, or 1/2 tablespoon fresh thyme
1/4	teaspoon pepper
1 3/4	cups chicken broth
3	tablespoons dry sherry
1/2	cup milk
2	cups chopped cooked chicken or turkey
1	(16-ounce) package frozen mixed vegetables without lima beans, or chopped fresh mixed vegetables

For the potpie, melt the butter in a large saucepan over low heat. Add the onion and sauté until translucent. Add the flour, salt, thyme and pepper. Cook until the mixture is smooth and bubbly, stirring constantly. Stir in the broth, sherry and milk. Bring to a boil, stirring constantly. Cook for 1 minute, stirring constantly. Stir in the chicken and vegetables. Remove from the heat. Preheat the oven to 425 degrees. Roll two-thirds of the pastry into a 13-inch square on a lightly floured surface. Fit into a 9×9-inch baking pan. Pour the filling into the pastry-lined pan. Roll the remaining pastry into an 11-inch square. Place over the filling, rolling under the edges and fluting. Cut slits in the center to allow steam to escape. Bake for 30 to 35 minutes or until the crust is golden brown. Remove from the oven and let stand for 5 to 8 minutes before serving.

Serves 6

CHICKEN SHISH KABOBS

1 1/2 cups vegetable oil

3/4 cup soy sauce

1/2 cup red wine vinegar

1/3 cup fresh lemon juice

1/4 cup Worcestershire sauce

2 tablespoons dry mustard

2 1/4 teaspoons salt

1 tablespoon freshly
ground pepper

2 garlic cloves, minced

2 to 5 pounds boneless skinless
chicken breasts

1 to 3 pounds white or brown
whole mushrooms

1 or 2 large red onions

3 to 6 large green bell peppers
or red bell peppers

3 to 6 small zucchini or yellow
squash (optional)

Mix the oil, soy sauce, vinegar, lemon juice, Worcestershire sauce, dry mustard, salt, pepper and garlic in a large sealable plastic bag. Cut the chicken into pieces large enough to be skewered. Add to the marinade and seal the bag, turning to coat. Marinate in the refrigerator for 2 to 3 hours.

Cut the mushrooms, onions, bell peppers and zucchini into pieces large enough to be skewered. Preheat the grill. Drain the chicken, discarding the marinade. Thread the chicken and vegetables separately onto skewers. Place on a grill rack. Grill until the chicken is cooked through and the vegetables are tender.

Serves 6 to 8

The marinade is the secret behind this mouthwatering dish. This marinade is also outstanding with pork, beef, and any variety of vegetables. Serve the shish kabobs over the RealSalt Lemon Rice on page 174.

CHICKEN PASTA WITH HAM AND SUN-DRIED TOMATOES

4 to 6 boneless skinless
chicken breasts, chopped

2 garlic cloves, minced
Olive oil

2 cups coarsely chopped,
zucchini

1 (1/4-inch-thick) slice ham,
cut into 1-inch long strips

4 cups heavy whipping cream

1 cup (1/4-inch strips) sun-dried
tomatoes

2 pounds penne or ziti, cooked
and drained

Sauté the chicken and garlic in a small amount of olive oil in a skillet until the chicken is cooked through. Sauté the zucchini and ham in a small amount of olive oil in a skillet until the zucchini is tender. Heat a large heavy skillet until hot. Pour enough olive oil into the hot skillet to coat the bottom. Add the whipping cream. Boil for several minutes or until golden brown and thickened, stirring constantly. Stir in the chicken mixture and ham mixture. Cook until heated through. Stir in the sun-dried tomatoes. Spoon over the hot pasta in a large bowl and serve.

Serves 6

PESTO CHICKEN WITH PENNE

1/4 teaspoon olive oil

4 ounces boneless skinless
chicken breasts, cut into
1-inch pieces

1 green onion, chopped

1 (13-ounce) can water-pack
artichoke hearts, drained
and sliced

1 tablespoon basil pesto

1 tablespoon light sour cream

2 ounces whole wheat pasta,
cooked and drained

1 tablespoon grated
Parmesan cheese

Spray a skillet with nonstick cooking spray and add the olive oil. Heat over medium heat. Add the chicken. Cook for 4 to 5 minutes or until cooked through. Remove the chicken to a plate. Add the green onion to the drippings in the skillet. Sauté for 1 to 2 minutes. Add the artichoke hearts, pesto and sour cream and mix well. Return the chicken to the skillet. Add the pasta and toss to coat. Sprinkle with the cheese.

Serves 1

Pasta with Chicken and Sun-Dried Tomatoes

3	cups penne
1/2	cup chopped oil-pack sun-dried tomatoes
4	garlic cloves, minced
2	large chicken breasts, chopped
1/4	cup chopped prosciutto
1/4	cup pecans, chopped
1/2	cup chicken broth
1/2	cup crumbled feta cheese

Cook the pasta in a large saucepan using the package directions; drain. Heat the sun-dried tomatoes in a large skillet until the oil is heated through. Remove the sun-dried tomatoes to a small bowl. Drain the skillet, reserving 1 teaspoon of the oil in the skillet. Add the garlic and chicken to the reserved oil. Cook until the chicken is almost cooked through. Add the sun-dried tomatoes, prosciutto, pecans and broth and cook until the chicken is cooked through. Add the chicken mixture to the pasta in a bowl and toss to coat. Add the cheese and toss until slightly melted.

Serves 8

Chicken Stir-Fry Lettuce Cups

1	large yellow onion
1	large red bell pepper
1 1/2	pounds boneless skinless chicken breasts, thinly sliced
	Salt and pepper to taste
2	tablespoons extra-virgin olive oil
3	garlic cloves, minced
1 1/2	teaspoons grated fresh ginger
1/4	teaspoon red pepper flakes
3	tablespoons low-sodium soy sauce
3	tablespoons rice wine vinegar
1 1/2	teaspoons cornstarch
1	tablespoon water
12	to 16 leaves Boston lettuce

Cut the onion into halves and thinly slice. Cut the bell pepper into thin slices. Sprinkle the chicken with salt and pepper. Heat 1 tablespoon of the olive oil in a skillet over high heat. Add one-half of the chicken. Cook for 2 to 4 minutes or until cooked through, stirring constantly. Remove to a plate. Repeat with the remaining chicken. Add the remaining 1 tablespoon olive oil, the onion and bell pepper to the skillet. Sauté for 4 minutes or until the onion is tender and golden, reducing the heat if browning too quickly. Reduce the heat to medium. Add the garlic, ginger and red pepper flakes. Cook for 1 minute or until fragrant, stirring constantly. Stir in the soy sauce, vinegar and a mixture of the cornstarch and water. Remove from the heat. Add the chicken and any accumulated drippings and toss lightly. Spoon into the lettuce leaves and serve.

Serves 4

THAI CHICKEN IN SPICY PEANUT SAUCE

1/2 large onion, coarsely chopped
    Olive oil
4   to 6 boneless skinless
    chicken breasts, cut into
    1/2-inch strips
1   cup chicken broth
1/4 cup soy sauce
1   tablespoon ground cumin
3   garlic cloves, minced
1/2 teaspoon red pepper flakes
    Salt and black pepper to taste
3   tablespoons cornstarch
1/2 cup creamy peanut butter
1   tablespoon soy sauce
    Juice of 1 lemon
1   large red bell pepper, seeded
    and cut into strips
1   bunch broccoli,
    cut into florets
1/2 bunch green onions, chopped
1/4 cup cilantro, chopped
1/2 cup roasted peanuts or
    cashews, chopped

Sauté the onion in a small amount of olive oil in a large saucepan for 2 minutes. Add the chicken. Sauté over medium heat for 5 minutes. Add the broth and 1/4 cup soy sauce and mix well. Stir in the cumin, garlic, red pepper flakes, salt and black pepper. Cook, covered, over low heat for 30 minutes.

Remove 1 cup of the liquid from the saucepan and mix with the cornstarch, peanut butter, 1 tablespoon soy sauce and the lemon juice in a bowl. Return to the saucepan and mix well. Cook, covered, over low heat for 15 to 30 minutes, adding the bell pepper and broccoli during the last 5 minutes. Sprinkle with the green onions, cilantro and peanuts before serving. Serve with hot cooked rice or noodles.

Serves 4 to 6

CILANTRO LIME CHICKEN FAJITAS

1 bunch cilantro

3/4 cup olive oil

5 tablespoons fresh lime juice (about 2 limes)

2 1/2 teaspoons ground cumin

1 1/2 teaspoons ancho chili powder

Salt and pepper to taste

6 boneless skinless chicken breasts

3 large poblano chiles or ancho chiles

3 large red, yellow or orange bell peppers

1 or 2 red onions

12 (8-inch) flour tortillas, warmed

Preheat the grill. Purée the cilantro, olive oil, lime juice, cumin and chili powder in a food processor or blender. Season with salt and pepper. Place the chicken in a glass dish. Pour one-half of the marinade over the chicken and turn to coat.

Remove the seeds from the chiles and cut the chiles lengthwise into 3/4-inch strips. Cut the bell peppers lengthwise into 3/4-inch strips. Cut the onions into 1/2-inch-thick slices. Combine the vegetables with the remaining marinade in a glass dish, turning to coat.

Remove the chicken from the marinade, discarding the marinade. Place the chicken on a grill rack. Grill over medium heat for 7 minutes on each side or until cooked through. Remove the vegetables from the marinade, discarding the marinade. Arrange the vegetables on a grill rack at the same time as the chicken. Grill the onions for 15 minutes and the chiles and bell peppers for 12 minutes or until the vegetables are tender and slightly blackened. Cut the chicken into strips. Fill the tortillas with the chicken and vegetables. Serve with sour cream, salsa and avocado.

Note: This marinade can be used with a variety of meats and vegetables.

Serves 6

SWEET POTATO CHICKEN CURRY

1 (14-ounce) can coconut milk
3 tablespoons red curry paste
2 tablespoons fish sauce
3 tablespoons brown sugar
1/3 cup water
2 large carrots, peeled and sliced
1 large sweet potato, peeled and chopped
1 red bell pepper, sliced
1/2 small green zucchini, sliced (optional)
1 to 1 1/2 large boneless chicken breasts, cut into bite-size pieces
1 cup frozen peas
Hot cooked jasmine rice

Simmer the coconut milk and curry paste in a large saucepan over medium heat for 5 minutes. Add the fish sauce, brown sugar and water. Simmer for 5 minutes. Add the carrots, sweet potato, bell pepper and zucchini. Cook for 8 minutes or until the vegetables are soft. Add the chicken. Simmer until the chicken is cooked through. Add the peas. Cook for 2 minutes. Spoon over hot rice to serve.

Serves 4

TURKEY VEGETABLE MEAT LOAF

1 small zucchini
1 large carrot
1/2 large yellow onion
1 pound ground turkey (breast and thigh mix)
1/2 cup bread crumbs
1 egg
1 tablespoon garlic salt
1 teaspoon pepper
1/2 cup ketchup

Preheat the oven to 400 degrees. Grate the zucchini, carrot and onion into a bowl. Add the ground turkey, bread crumbs, egg, garlic salt and pepper and mix by hand until loosely blended. Pack evenly into a 5X7-inch loaf pan sprayed with nonstick cooking spray. Spread the ketchup evenly over the top. Bake for 35 minutes or to 165 degrees on a meat thermometer. Remove from the oven. Cover and let stand for 10 minutes. Cut into slices and serve.

Serves 6

HERB SALT-RUBBED RACK OF LAMB WITH HONEY-VINEGAR REDUCTION

Honey-Vinegar Reduction

- 1/2 cup red wine vinegar
- 1/4 cup honey

Lamb

- 2 tablespoons kosher salt
- 3/4 teaspoon freshly ground pepper
- 1/4 cup packed Italian parsley leaves
- 1 tablespoon fresh thyme
- 2 teaspoons fresh rosemary
- 3 garlic cloves, coarsely chopped
- 1 1/2 tablespoons extra-virgin olive oil
- 2 (8-rib) frenched racks of lamb, trimmed of all but a thin layer of fat (each rack about 1 1/2 pounds)

For the reduction, mix the vinegar and honey in a small heavy saucepan. Bring to a simmer. Simmer for 20 to 25 minutes or until the mixture is reduced to 1/4 cup and is of a syrupy consistency.

For the lamb, pulse the kosher salt, pepper, parsley, thyme and rosemary eight to ten times in a food processor or blender to resemble a green salt. Add the garlic and olive oil and pulse one or two times. Rub the lamb racks liberally with the herb mixture. Cover with plastic wrap. Let rest in the refrigerator for 2 to 3 hours. Preheat the grill. Remove the plastic wrap from the lamb racks. Place the lamb racks in the middle of a grill rack. Grill for 10 to 12 minutes on each side or to 120 degrees on a meat thermometer for medium-rare. Remove to a platter and tent with foil. Let rest for 5 minutes. Cut each rack of lamb into individual chops and drizzle with the reduction.

Note: To roast the lamb, preheat the oven to 375 degrees. Place the lamb racks in the middle of a rack in a roasting pan and bake for 25 to 30 minutes or to the desired degree of doneness.

Serves 6

As the signature recipe of this book, this easy-to-prepare dish highlights three ingredients that Utah is most well known for: salt, honey, and lamb. Created by Utah chef RJ Peterson, this sweet and salty main course will delight guests and family alike. The honey-vinegar reduction elegantly enriches the flavor of the herb-salted lamb. Serve with roasted new potatoes and grilled seasonal vegetables.

MARGUERITE HENDERSON'S COFFEE AND SPICE LAMB KABOBS WITH LEMON MINT RICE

Lemon Mint Rice

- 2 tablespoons butter
- 1/4 cup chopped onion
- 1 cup long grain rice
- 2 cups vegetable stock or chicken stock
  Pinch of saffron (optional)
  Zest of 1 lemon
- 1/2 teaspoon kosher salt
- 1/8 teaspoon white pepper
- 1/2 cup fresh mint leaves, chopped
- 1/4 cup sliced almonds or pine nuts, toasted

For the rice, melt the butter in a medium saucepan. Add the onion. Sauté over medium heat for 2 minutes or until soft. Add the rice. Cook for 1 minute, stirring constantly. Add the stock, saffron, lemon zest, kosher salt and white pepper. Simmer, covered, for 20 minutes or until the rice is cooked through and the liquid is absorbed. Stir in the mint and almonds. Adjust the seasonings to taste.

Lamb Kabobs

- 1 (2 1/2- to 3-pound) boneless leg of lamb
- 1/2 cup coffee beans, finely ground
- 2 teaspoons cinnamon
- 1 teaspoon ground cumin
- 1 teaspoon ground allspice
- 1 tablespoon fennel seeds
- 2 garlic cloves, minced
- 1 teaspoon kosher salt
- 1/2 teaspoon coarsely ground pepper
- 2 tablespoons olive oil
  Zest and juice of 1 large lemon

For the kabobs, trim the lamb and cut into 1/2-inch pieces. Mix the ground coffee, cinnamon, cumin, allspice, fennel seeds, garlic, kosher salt, pepper, olive oil, lemon zest and lemon juice in a large bowl. Add the lamb and toss to coat. Marinate in the refrigerator for at least 30 minutes or up to 2 hours. Preheat the oven to 375 degrees. Thread three to six pieces of lamb onto twelve to twenty-four 6-inch wooden skewers or eight to ten metal skewers. Place on a rack in a roasting pan. Roast for 8 to 10 minutes or until the lamb pieces are pink in the center and not overcooked. Serve over the rice.

Note: If using wooden skewers, soak in water before using. To grill, preheat the grill. Place the kabobs on a grill rack and grill over medium heat for 4 to 5 minutes on each side.

Serves 4 to 6

SPICED MORGAN VALLEY LAMB SHOULDER CHOPS

4 Morgan Valley Lamb
 shoulder chops (blade
 or round bone),
 cut 3/4 inch thick
2 teaspoons lemon pepper
2 teaspoons garlic powder
2 teaspoons dried rosemary
 leaves, crushed
2 tablespoons olive oil
1 small red bell pepper,
 thinly sliced
1/2 cup chopped onion
3 garlic cloves, finely chopped
1/4 cup slivered almonds
1/4 cup chopped fresh basil
1 tablespoon red wine vinegar
1/2 teaspoon freshly ground salt
1/2 teaspoon freshly ground
 pepper

Sprinkle the lamb with the lemon pepper, garlic powder and rosemary. Heat 1 1/2 tablespoons of the olive oil in a large skillet. Add the chops. Cook until brown on each side and to the desired degree of doneness. Remove to a heatproof platter. Cover and keep warm.

Wipe out the skillet and then pour in the remaining 1/2 tablespoon olive oil. Add the bell pepper, onion and garlic. Sauté for 3 to 4 minutes or until soft. Add the almonds, basil, vinegar, salt and pepper. Sauté for 2 to 3 minutes or until the almonds are toasted. Spoon over the chops and serve.

Serves 4

Utahans are fortunate to have a fine lamb purveyor right on their doorstep—Morgan Valley Lamb, whose motto echoes their sustainable approach: "Fresh air, clean water, and wholesome forage make the best lamb."

TAPENADE LAMB KABOBS AND COUSCOUS

Lamb

3/4 cup (1 1/2 sticks) butter, softened

3 anchovy fillets

3 garlic cloves

1 teaspoon lemon zest

1/8 teaspoon red pepper flakes

1 teaspoon kosher salt

1 teaspoon freshly ground black pepper

1 cup kalamata olives, pitted

1 tablespoon capers

2 pounds round lamb, cut into 1 1/2- to 2-inch pieces

1 to 2 tablespoons olive oil

1 to 2 tablespoons herbes de Provence

1 teaspoon kosher salt

1 teaspoon ground black pepper

Couscous

1 teaspoon butter

1 garlic clove, minced

2 cups chicken stock

1 cup couscous

1 cup spinach chiffonade

1/4 cup pine nuts

2 tablespoons chopped parsley
Kosher salt and freshly ground pepper to taste

For the lamb, process the butter, anchovies, garlic, lemon zest, red pepper flakes, 1 teaspoon kosher salt and 1 teaspoon black pepper in a food processor until smooth. Add the olives and capers and pulse until chopped. Place in a bowl. Chill, covered with plastic wrap, for 1 hour or longer. Preheat the grill to medium-high. Toss the lamb with the olive oil in a bowl to coat. Thread loosely onto skewers. Sprinkle with the herbes de Provence, 1 teaspoon kosher salt and 1 teaspoon black pepper and pat to adhere. Place on a grill rack. Grill for 10 to 15 minutes for medium-rare or to the desired degree of doneness, turning two to three times. Place on a platter. Top each kabob with about 1 tablespoon of the tapenade butter. Cover with foil and let rest for 5 minutes.

For the couscous, melt the butter in a small saucepan over medium heat. Add the garlic and sauté for 30 seconds. Add the stock and bring to a boil. Stir in the couscous. Cover and remove from the heat. Let stand for 10 minutes. Sauté the pine nuts in a small sauté pan over medium-low heat until toasted and just beginning to turn golden. Fluff the couscous with a fork. Add the spinach, pine nuts, parsley, kosher salt and pepper. Serve with the kabobs.

Serves 4

GOLDENER HIRSCH INN'S DUCK CONFIT WITH RIESLING CHOUCROUTE

Riesling Choucroute

1 1/2	cups	chopped pancetta
2	heads	red cabbage, julienned
2	cups	sweet riesling
1 1/2	cups	apple cider vinegar
1/2	tablespoon	crushed toasted caraway seeds
1/2	tablespoon	crushed toasted fennel seeds
		Kosher salt and freshly ground pepper to taste
1/2	cup	chopped Italian parsley

Duck

1/4	cup	kosher salt
4		whole cloves
1	tablespoon	brown sugar
1	teaspoon	crushed caraway seeds
1	teaspoon	dry mustard
6		Peking duck legs (5 pounds)
3	cups	rendered duck fat

Award-winning Goldener Hirsch Inn Restaurant at Deer Valley Resort in Park City, Utah, serves contemporary Alpine cuisine with an American spin. This recipe is surprisingly easy for the home chef to prepare.

For the choucroute, render the pancetta in a large heavy saucepan over medium to high heat until the fat is light brown. Remove the pancetta with a slotted spoon to a bowl, reserving the drippings in the saucepan. Add the cabbage to the reserved drippings. Cook over medium heat until limp. Add the wine. Cook until the liquid has evaporated. Add the vinegar. Cook until the liquid has evaporated. Add the pancetta, caraway seeds and fennel seeds and mix well. Sprinkle with kosher salt and pepper. Let stand until completely cool. Fold in the parsley. Store in an airtight container in the refrigerator. You may substitute pepper bacon for the pancetta, if desired.

For the duck, mix the kosher salt, cloves, brown sugar, caraway seeds and dry mustard in a bowl. Spread liberally over both sides of the duck. Chill for 12 hours or longer. Preheat the oven to 200 degrees. Melt the duck fat in a small saucepan. Rinse the spice mix from the duck and pat dry. Place the duck in a large deep baking pan. Pour the duck fat over the duck. Cover with foil and seal completely. Bake for 6 to 8 hours or until the skin has shrunk, leaving most of the leg bone exposed and the thigh meat can be depressed with a little pressure from your thumb.

To serve, increase the oven temperature to 400 degrees. Place the duck skin side up in a baking pan. Bake until heated through and the skin is light brown. Reheat the riesling choucroute in a sauté pan until heated through. Place on individual serving plates and top each with a duck leg. Rendered duck fat can be found at stores such as Williams-Sonoma, Whole Foods, or other fine food purveyors.

Serves 6

Log Haven Quinoa-Crusted Crab Cakes

Crab Cakes

- 1 pound shrimp
- 2 large egg whites
- 1 pound Dungeness crab meat
- 1/2 cup mayonnaise
- 2 tablespoons Dijon mustard
- Juice of 1 or 2 lemons
- 2 to 3 tablespoons chopped Italian parsley
- Cayenne pepper to taste
- Salt and black pepper to taste
- 1 cup toasted cooked quinoa

Frisée Salad

- 1 butternut squash
- 1/4 cup drawn butter
- Salt and black pepper to taste
- 1/3 cup grapeseed oil
- 1 to 2 tablespoons Meyer lemon juice
- 1 teaspoon Dijon mustard
- 3 tablespoons apple juice concentrate
- 1 or 2 medium shallots, chopped
- 1 sprig of fresh thyme
- 1 tablespoon chopped Italian parsley
- Dash of cayenne pepper
- 2 heads baby frisée, rinsed
- 1 large apple, chopped
- 3 tablespoons hazelnuts, toasted and chopped

For the crab cakes, preheat the oven to 400 degrees. Peel the shrimp. Remove the tails and devein. Purée the shrimp and egg whites in a food processor. Combine the crab meat, mayonnaise, Dijon mustard, lemon juice, parsley, cayenne pepper, salt and black pepper in a bowl and mix lightly. Add the puréed shrimp mixture and mix well. Divide the crab meat mixture into six portions. Shape each portion into a patty. Process the quinoa, salt and pepper in a food processor. Dredge the patties in the quinoa mixture. Cook in a nonstick skillet until golden brown. Place on a baking sheet. Bake for 3 to 4 minutes or until heated through.

For the salad, cut the squash into disks about 1/3 inch thick. Sauté the squash in the butter in a skillet until soft. Sprinkle with salt and pepper. Whisk the oil, lemon juice, Dijon mustard, apple juice concentrate, shallots, thyme, parsley, cayenne pepper, salt and black pepper together in a bowl. Toss the frisée, apple and hazelnuts together in a salad bowl. Add the desired amount of the dressing and toss to coat. Divide the butternut squash among six serving plates. Top each with a crab cake and some of the frisée salad.

Serves 6

For more than eighty years, Log Haven, nestled in Salt Lake City's Millcreek Canyon, has been a treasured destination for celebrations and special events. Log Haven focuses on local and world-class cuisine and has consistently been voted one of the most romantic places to dine along the Wasatch Front.

MEDITRINA'S CURRY LIME PRAWNS

1 tablespoon yellow
 curry powder
2 teaspoons ground cumin
1/2 teaspoon cayenne pepper
1/4 teaspoon ground ginger
1 tablespoon sugar
1/2 teaspoon salt
3 tablespoons fresh lime juice
1 tablespoon butter
1 1/2 cups half-and-half
1/4 cup extra-virgin olive oil or
 canola oil
1 1/2 pounds deveined
 peeled prawns

Whisk the curry powder, cumin, cayenne pepper, ginger, sugar, salt, lime juice and butter in a saucepan over medium heat until the butter melts. Add the half-and-half. Bring to a boil. Reduce the heat and simmer for 3 to 5 minutes. Remove from the heat. Heat the olive oil in a large sauté pan over medium-high heat. Add the prawns. Cook until the prawns almost turn pink, stirring constantly. Add the sauce and cook for 1 minute longer. Do not overcook.

Serves 4 to 6

Meditrina, a Spanish tapas bar in Salt Lake City, creates dishes with fresh, local ingredients. This gluten-free dish is one of its specialties. Serve over basmati rice for an entrée or on cucumber slices for an appetizer. The sauce may also be used on chicken or fish.

TIGER PRAWNS WITH TOMATOES AND PASTA

12 ounces whole wheat pasta
6   tablespoons olive oil
4   garlic cloves, minced
12 to 15 large tiger prawns,
    peeled and deveined
2   cups yellow teardrop
    tomatoes or grape tomatoes,
    cut into halves
6   basil leaves, shredded
    Shredded Parmesan cheese
    Salt and pepper to taste

Cook the pasta using the package directions. Heat the olive oil in a large skillet over medium-high heat. Add the garlic and sauté for 1 minute. Add the prawns. Cook for 5 minutes or until the prawns turn pink. Drain the pasta. Toss with the tomatoes in a large bowl. Add the prawns, basil, cheese, salt and pepper and toss to coat, adding additional olive oil 1 teaspoon at a time if needed.

Note: Asparagus or zucchini may be sautéed with the shrimp. Feta cheese or goat cheese may be used instead of the Parmesan cheese.

Serves 2

SHRIMP WITH LEMON HERB BUTTER SAUCE

8   ounces angel hair pasta
     Salt to taste
     Olive oil
12   ounces shrimp, peeled
     and deveined
2   garlic cloves, chopped
1   shallot, minced
4   tablespoons butter
1/4 cup rice vinegar
1/4 cup white wine
1/2 cup chicken broth
2   teaspoons thyme
     Zest and juice from 1 lemon
1   Roma tomato, chopped
1   tablespoon minced chives
2   tablespoons minced parsley
     White pepper to taste

Cook the pasta in boiling salted water in a saucepan until al dente. Drain and drizzle with olive oil to prevent sticking together.

Cook the shrimp, garlic and shallot in 1 tablespoon of the butter in a large nonstick skillet until the shrimp turn pink. Remove from the heat.

Boil the vinegar, wine, broth and thyme in a small saucepan until thickened and reduced to about 1/2 cup. Reduce the heat to low. Whisk in the remaining 3 tablespoons butter 1 tablespoon at a time. Do not let the butter boil. Add the lemon zest, lemon juice, tomato, chives, parsley, salt and white pepper and mix well. Keep warm.

Return the shrimp mixture to low heat. Add the pasta and three-fourths of the sauce and toss to mix. Serve on large plates or in large pasta bowls. Drizzle with the remaining sauce.

Serves 4

GARLIC AND GINGER SHRIMP WITH RICE NOODLES

8 ounces rice noodles

2 to 2 1/2 pounds fresh jumbo shrimp

1 (2-inch) piece of fresh ginger

9 or 10 green onions

1/2 small red bell pepper

1/2 small orange bell pepper

1/2 small yellow bell pepper

2 tablespoons olive oil

4 garlic cloves, finely chopped

3 red chiles, finely chopped

1 cup broccoli florets

2 tablespoons lemon juice

1/2 cup white wine, or more to taste

1 teaspoon brown sugar

2 teaspoons fish sauce

1 bunch cilantro, chopped

Cover the noodles with boiling water in a heatproof bowl. Soak for 8 minutes; drain and set aside. Remove the tails and devein the shrimp. Julienne the ginger. Cut the green onions into short lengths. Thinly slice the bell peppers. Heat a large wok until hot. Spoon in the olive oil and swirl to coat. Add the shrimp, garlic, ginger and chiles in two batches and stir-fry until the shrimp turn pink, removing to a warm platter after each addition. Combine the green onions, bell peppers and broccoli in the hot wok. Stir-fry over high heat for 2 to 3 minutes or until partially cooked through. Add the lemon juice, wine and brown sugar. Cook until the liquid is reduced by two-thirds. Return the shrimp to the wok. Sprinkle with the fish sauce. Stir-fry until heated through. Sprinkle with the cilantro. Serve with the noodles.

Serves 4 to 6

Foil-Baked Halibut

2 pounds halibut fillets
1 onion, sliced
3 tablespoons mayonnaise
  Juice of 1 lime
  Dash of Worcestershire sauce
  Dash of soy sauce
2 tablespoons butter

Preheat the oven to 350 degrees. Arrange the fish on a large sheet of foil. Top with the onion. Combine the mayonnaise, lime juice, Worcestershire sauce and soy sauce in a bowl and mix well. Pour over the fish. Dot with the butter. Seal the foil to form a packet. Bake for 20 to 25 minutes or until the fish flakes easily.

Note: To grill, place the fish packet on a grill rack. Grill for 20 to 25 minutes or until the fish flakes easily.

Serves 4

Squatters' Captain Bastard's Stout Salmon

1 (12-ounce) bottle Captain Bastard's oatmeal stout
6 tablespoons rice wine vinegar
1/2 teaspoon Worcestershire sauce
2 tablespoons minced garlic
2 tablespoons minced ginger
1 tablespoon cracked pepper
6 (8-ounce) salmon fillets
1/2 cup caramelized onions

Combine the beer, vinegar, Worcestershire sauce, garlic, ginger and pepper in a bowl and mix well. Place the fish in a sealable plastic bag. Add the marinade and seal the bag. Marinate in the refrigerator for 8 to 12 hours. Drain the fish, discarding the marinade. Sauté the fish in a nonstick skillet over medium heat until opaque. Serve over the caramelized onions.

Note: The fish may also be grilled.

Serves 4

The priority at Squatters Brew Pub is to support the local community. Squatters' sustainability focused business model centers on recycling, being resource-wise with water and electricity, partnering with local food purveyors, and brewing a certified organic beer—Organic Amber Ale. Although this dish calls for Captain Bastard's Oatmeal Stout, a similarly robust beer may be substituted. Experiment with other microbrews available in your area.

CEDAR-PLANKED SALMON WITH CHEF'S DRESSING

Chef's Dressing

- 1 cup mayonnaise
- 1/4 cup chopped fresh basil
- 1/4 cup chopped fresh parsley
- 3 green onions, chopped
  Zest from 1 small lemon
- 1 teaspoon hot pepper sauce, or to taste

Salmon

- 4 salmon fillets
- 2 tablespoons unsalted butter, melted
- 1 teaspoon whole mustard seeds
- 1 teaspoon dried dill weed
- 1 teaspoon salt
- 1/2 teaspoon white pepper
- 1 teaspoon sugar
- 1 teaspoon paprika
- 1 teaspoon granulated onion powder

For the dressing, combine the mayonnaise, basil, parsley, green onions, lemon zest and hot sauce in a bowl and mix well. The dressing will be chunky.

For the fish, submerge two medium cedar planks completely in water in a large pan. Soak for 30 minutes or longer; drain. Preheat the grill. Brush the fish with the butter. Mix the mustard seeds, dill weed, salt, white pepper, sugar, paprika and onion powder in a bowl. Sprinkle lightly over the fish. Place two fish fillets on each plank. Grill over indirect medium heat for 10 minutes or to the desired degree of doneness. Remove the fish from the planks and let rest for 5 minutes. Serve with a small dollop of the dressing on the side.

Serves 4

Pacific Salmon with Roasted Red Pepper Beurre Pomme

2 tablespoons extra-virgin
    olive oil
4 (8-ounce) Pacific salmon fillets
1 shallot, finely chopped
1/2 cup finely chopped roasted
    red pepper
2 cups apple juice, or 1/2 cup
    100 percent apple juice
    concentrate
    Juice of 1 large lemon
2 tablespoons butter,
    cut into 8 pieces
    Salt to taste

Heat a skillet over medium-high heat. Spoon in 1 tablespoon of the olive oil and swirl in the skillet. Add the fish. Spoon the remaining 1 tablespoon olive oil over the top. Cook until the center of the fish is beginning to turn opaque and firm, turning once. Remove the fish to a warm platter, reserving the drippings in the skillet. Let rest in a warm place for 10 minutes.

Sauté the shallot and roasted pepper in the reserved drippings over high heat until the shallot is translucent. Add the apple juice and lemon juice. Cook over high heat until the liquid is almost completely evaporated. Reduce the heat to low. Whisk in two pats of the butter at a time until melted. Sprinkle with salt. Place the fish on individual serving plates and top with the sauce.

Note: Use one-half of a 12-ounce jar of roasted red peppers packed in brine as a time saver. This recipe is great served with steamed broccoli sprinkled with lemon pepper.

Serves 4

FISH TACOS

3 tablespoons extra-virgin
 olive oil

4 garlic cloves, minced

1 serrano chile, seeded
 and minced

3/4 teaspoon sweet paprika

1 teaspoon pepper

8 (6-ounce) skinless red
 snapper fillets or
 tilapia fillets

1 cup shredded green cabbage

1 cup shredded red cabbage

1/4 cup minced red onion

1 cup cilantro

1/4 cup plain yogurt

1/4 cup mayonnaise

2 tablespoons fresh lime juice
 Salt and pepper to taste

2 large ripe avocados
 Lime juice for sprinkling

24 (6-inch) corn tortillas

Mix the olive oil, garlic, serrano chile, paprika and 1 teaspoon pepper in a small bowl. Rub over the fish in a large glass dish. Chill, covered, for 30 minutes to 4 hours. Combine the green cabbage, red cabbage, onion and cilantro in a bowl and mix well. Process the yogurt, mayonnaise, 2 tablespoons lime juice and salt and pepper to taste in a blender or food processor until smooth. Cut the avocados into slices and sprinkle with lime juice.

Preheat the grill. Season the fish with salt and pepper to taste. Place on a grill rack. Grill over medium heat for 3 minutes on each side or just until cooked through. Remove to a platter. Tear into large chunks and cover with foil. Wrap three stacks of eight tortillas each in foil. Place on the grill rack. Grill for 5 minutes or until heated through. Stack two tortillas on each serving plate. Spoon a heaping tablespoonful of the fish, a small handful of the cabbage mixture and a couple of avocado slices on each tortilla stack. Top each with 1 tablespoon of the yogurt mixture and a sprinkle of lime juice. Serve with a side of Mexican rice and slices of fresh mangoes or papayas.

Note: To bake the tortillas, preheat the oven to 350 degrees. Wrap in foil as directed above and bake for 10 minutes. They may also be fried in one-quarter inch of hot vegetable oil until lightly golden but not crispy and then drained on paper towels. You may substitute 1/4 cup sour cream for the yogurt or mayonnaise, or use a combination of all three, if desired.

Serves 6 to 8

Citrus Fish

1   tablespoon vegetable oil
1   (1-pound) white fish fillet
    Pinch of salt
    Pinch of pepper
1   large lemon, cut into halves
1   large orange, cut into halves

Heat the oil in a large skillet. Sprinkle the fish with salt and pepper. Place in the hot skillet. Squeeze one-half of the lemon and one-half of the orange over the fish and place the citrus halves in the skillet cut side down. Cook for 5 to 6 minutes. Turn the fish. Repeat with the remaining lemon and orange halves. Cook for 5 to 6 minutes or until the fish flakes easily.

Serves 4

Tilapia in a Parmesan Cheese Sauce

1/2   cup (2 ounces) grated
      Parmesan cheese
1/4   cup (1/2 stick) butter,
      softened
3   tablespoons light mayonnaise
2   tablespoons fresh lemon juice
1/4   teaspoon dried basil
1/4   teaspoon pepper
1/8   teaspoon onion powder
1/8   teaspoon celery salt
4   tilapia fillets

Preheat the broiler. Line a baking sheet with foil and spray with nonstick cooking spray. Mix the cheese, butter, mayonnaise, lemon juice, basil, pepper, onion power and celery salt in a bowl and mix well. Place the fish 1/2 inch apart on the prepared baking sheet. Broil a few inches from the heat source for 3 minutes. Turn the fish and broil for 3 minutes longer. Remove from the oven. Cover the fish with the cheese sauce. Broil for 2 minutes or until the sauce is light brown and the fish flakes easily.

Serves 4

BLACK BEAN AND GOAT CHEESE ENCHILADAS

Tomatillo Salsa

4	or 5 tomatillos
1/2	cup chicken broth
2	garlic cloves
1/2	yellow onion, chopped
1	serrano chile, seeded
1	tablespoon chopped fresh cilantro

Enchiladas

1/4	cup chicken broth
1	cup cooked black beans
1	garlic clove, minced
1	serrano chile, minced
1/4	cup chopped fresh mango or papaya
2	scallion bulbs, thinly sliced
1/4	cup corn kernels (optional)
1/4	cup goat cheese
	Salt to taste
1/4	cup corn oil
4	(6-inch) corn tortillas

For the salsa, remove the husks from the tomatillos. Chop the tomatillos and place in a saucepan. Add the broth, garlic, onion and serrano chile and mix well. Cook over medium-high heat for 10 minutes, stirring frequently. Process with the cilantro in a food processor until smooth.

For the enchiladas, combine the broth, beans, garlic, serrano chile, mango, scallion bulbs and corn in a medium saucepan and mix well. Bring to a boil. Whisk in the goat cheese. Sprinkle with salt.

Heat the corn oil in a skillet until smoking. Heat the tortillas in the oil one at a time until moistened. Place between paper towels to drain. Spoon the bean mixture onto each tortilla and roll up to enclose the filling. Place seam side down on serving plates. Spoon the salsa over the top of each tortilla and garnish with chopped red bell pepper.

Note: If tomatillos are not available, use fresh or canned green tomatoes.

Serves 2

STIR-FRIED BOK CHOY AND SHIITAKE MUSHROOMS

3 dried shiitake mushrooms

1/2 cup boiling water

1/4 cup rice wine or other
white wine

3 tablespoons soy sauce

1/2 teaspoon chili garlic sauce, or
a pinch of cayenne pepper

1 tablespoon honey

2 tablespoons arrowroot
powder or cornstarch

1 large bunch bok choy

1 tablespoon canola oil

1 tablespoon sesame oil

3 garlic cloves, chopped

1 tablespoon chopped or grated
fresh ginger

Sriracha sauce to taste

Place the mushrooms in a heatproof bowl. Add the boiling water. Let stand until the mushrooms are rehydrated and soft. Drain the mushrooms, reserving the liquid. Chop the mushrooms into thin pieces. Mix the reserved mushroom liquid, wine, soy sauce, chili garlic sauce and honey in a cup or small bowl. Stir in the arrowroot powder with a fork.

Chop the bok choy. Heat the canola oil and sesame oil in a wok or large saucepan over high heat. Stir-fry the bok choy in the hot oil. Reduce the heat. Steam, covered, for 1 to 2 minutes. Add the chopped mushrooms, garlic, ginger, the wine mixture and Sriracha sauce. Stir-fry until the sauce thickens into a glaze. Remove from the heat. Serve with noodles or rice.

Note: You may add tofu or tempeh and additional vegetables like broccoli, green beans, snap peas, etc. Add at the same time as the mushrooms and then stir-fry until tender-crisp.

Serves 4

Vegetarian Tikka Masala

5 small yellow potatoes

1 tablespoon vegetable oil

1 small yellow onion, sliced

1 tablespoon minced
  fresh ginger

2 garlic cloves, minced

1 (32-ounce) can tomato sauce

1 tablespoon ground cumin

1 tablespoon garam masala

1 teaspoon red chili powder

1 small zucchini, sliced

1 small yellow squash, sliced

1 cup (or less) heavy cream

1 (15-ounce) can garbanzo beans

1 teaspoon chopped cilantro

Salt to taste

Chop the potatoes. Parboil in water in a saucepan; drain. Heat the oil in a saucepan over medium heat. Add the onion. Sauté until tender and translucent. Add the ginger and garlic. Sauté for 3 to 4 minutes. Add the tomato sauce, cumin, garam masala and chili powder and mix well. Add the potatoes. Simmer, covered, for 15 minutes, stirring occasionally. Add the zucchini and squash. Simmer for 5 to 10 minutes or until the vegetables are tender. Add the cream and beans. Cook over medium heat for 5 minutes. Stir in the cilantro and salt. Serve with hot cooked brown basmati rice.

Serves 4

Orecchiette with Fresh Mozzarella Cheese

10 ounces orecchiette
   Kosher salt to taste

16 ounces mini mozzarella balls

16 ounces red and yellow grape
   tomatoes or pear tomatoes

8 to 10 tablespoons extra-virgin
   olive oil

6 to 8 tablespoons white
   balsamic vinegar

5 tablespoons minced chives

1/4 cup minced fresh oregano
   Freshly ground pepper to taste

Cook the pasta in boiling salted water using the package directions. Drain and rinse with cold water to stop the cooking process. Combine the pasta, cheese, tomatoes, olive oil, vinegar, chives, oregano, kosher salt and pepper to taste and toss to coat.

Note: You may use garlic chives or regular chives.

Serves 4

ON THE SIDE

Coconut Curry Cashew Quinoa 172 • Sweet and Nutty Quinoa 173
Spinach Couscous Sauté 173 • Coconut Lime Risotto 174 • RealSalt Lemon Rice 174
Mexican Rice with Cilantro Dressing 175 • Wild Rice Casserole 176
Mushroom Barley 176 • Cheese Hominy Grits 177 • Sausage Stuffing 177
Sautéed Brussels Sprouts with Hazelnuts 179 • Festive Holiday Green Beans 179
Barbecued Beans 180 • Broccolini 180 • Marinated Beets 181
Greens with Cannellini Beans and Winter Squash 182 • Sautéed Kale or Collards 183
Roasted Carrots and Shallots 183 • Dutch Oven Potatoes 184 • Leek and Potato Gratin 184
Creamy au Gratin Potatoes 185 • Potato Gratin with Smoked Gouda 186
Potato Soufflé 186 • Indian-Style Potatoes (Aloo Subji) 187 • Butternut Squash Gratin 189
Sweet Potato Casserole 190 • Zucchini Fans 191 • Baked Basil Tomatoes 191
Roasted Cherry Tomatoes 192 • Baked Vegetables with Sour Cream 192
Parker House Rolls 193

COCONUT CURRY CASHEW QUINOA

3 tablespoons coconut oil

2 garlic cloves, chopped

1/2 teaspoon ground cumin

3 tablespoons curry powder

1/2 teaspoon fine sea salt

3 tablespoons whole
   wheat flour

2 cups vegetable stock

1 cup coconut milk

1 large tomato, chopped

1 cup chopped carrots

1 cup baby bella mushrooms

1 cup uncooked quinoa

1 cup cashews

Heat the coconut oil in a saucepan over medium heat until melted. Add the garlic. Cook for 4 to 5 minutes. Add the cumin, curry powder and sea salt and mix well. Stir in the flour gradually. Add the stock gradually, stirring constantly. Stir in the coconut milk, tomato, carrots and mushrooms. Simmer over low heat for 30 minutes, stirring every couple minutes. Cook the quinoa using the package directions. Spoon the sauce over the quinoa and sprinkle with the cashews.

Serves 4

Sweet and Nutty Quinoa

1 cup quinoa
1/2 tablespoon olive oil
1 large shallot, chopped, or
   1/4 cup chopped red onion
2 cups chicken broth
1/2 teaspoon salt
1/2 teaspoon black pepper
1/2 cup dried cranberries or
   dried currants
2 teaspoons fresh lemon zest
2 teaspoons fresh orange zest
1/2 cup slivered almonds or
   pine nuts
1 teaspoon red pepper flakes,
   or to taste

Rinse the quinoa in cold water. Heat the olive oil in a skillet over medium heat. Add the shallot and sauté until soft. Add the quinoa. Sauté for 2 to 3 minutes, stirring constantly. Add the broth, salt, black pepper and dried cranberries. Cook, covered, over low heat for 25 to 30 minutes or until the liquid is absorbed and the quinoa is soft. Spoon into a serving bowl. Add the lemon zest, orange zest, almonds and red pepper flakes and toss well. Serve hot or cold.

Serves 6 to 8

Spinach Couscous Sauté

1 teaspoon olive oil
1 onion, chopped
1 red bell pepper, chopped
2 garlic cloves, minced
1 cup chicken broth
1 cup marinara sauce
6 ounces baby spinach leaves,
   chopped
1 cup Israeli couscous

Heat the olive oil in a large skillet over medium heat. Add the onion, bell pepper and garlic. Sauté for 5 minutes or until soft, adding 1/4 cup of the broth after 3 to 4 minutes to keep moist. Stir in the remaining 3/4 cup broth and the marinara sauce. Cook for 2 minutes. Add the spinach and couscous. Cook, covered, for 5 minutes or until the couscous is cooked through and the spinach is wilted.

Serves 4

Coconut Lime Risotto

1 (12-ounce) can coconut milk
Juice of 1 lime
1 cup chicken stock
1/2 yellow onion, minced
1 garlic clove, minced
1 tablespoon olive oil
1 cup arborio rice
Salt to taste

Blend the coconut milk, lime juice and stock in a bowl. Cook the onion and garlic in the olive oil in a saucepan over medium-high heat until the onion is translucent. Do not brown. Stir in the rice.

Cook until the rice turns white, stirring constantly. Add just enough of the coconut milk mixture to cover the rice without rising above it. Cook until absorbed, stirring frequently. Repeat the process until the rice is al dente. The entire cooking time will be about 45 minutes. Sprinkle with salt. Garnish with grated nutmeg.

Serves 4 to 6

RealSalt Lemon Rice

5 cups hot cooked brown rice
or wild rice
1/2 cup fresh lemon juice
1/4 cup (1/2 stick) butter
Leaves from 1 bunch Italian
parsley, chopped
2 teaspoons Redmond RealSalt
garlic salt, or to taste

Combine the hot brown rice, lemon juice, butter, parsley and 2 teaspoons garlic salt in a bowl and mix well. Add garlic salt to taste.

Serves 6

Mexican Rice with Cilantro Dressing

Cilantro Dressing

1 1/4 cups packed chopped cilantro
(about 1 small bunch)

3/4 cup olive oil

3 tablespoons cider vinegar

3 tablespoons red wine vinegar

2 garlic cloves, chopped

1 teaspoon ground cumin

1 teaspoon minced seeded
serrano chile

Salt and pepper to taste

Rice

1 tablespoon olive oil

1 large white or yellow
onion, chopped

2 garlic cloves, chopped

1/2 (4-ounce) can chopped mild
green chiles

2 cups long grain white rice

3 1/2 cups chicken broth
without MSG

Salt and pepper to taste

For the dressing, process the cilantro, olive oil, cider vinegar, red wine vinegar, garlic, cumin and serrano chile in a blender or food processor until smooth. Season with salt and pepper. Chill, covered, for up to 1 day.

For the rice, heat the olive oil in a large saucepan over medium heat. Add the onion, garlic and green chiles. Cook over medium heat for 5 to 10 minutes or until the onion is soft. Stir in the rice. Cook for 2 minutes, stirring constantly. Stir in the broth and bring to a boil. Reduce the heat to low. Cook, covered, for 15 minutes or until the rice is tender and the liquid is absorbed. Turn off the heat. Let stand, covered, for 5 minutes. Spoon into a serving bowl. Let stand for 5 minutes longer to cool slightly. Pour the dressing over the rice, tossing gently. Season with salt and pepper.

Note: This recipe may be prepared in advance. Bring to room temperature before serving.

Serves 8

WILD RICE CASSEROLE

1	pound smoked sausage
1	cup chopped celery
1/2	cup chopped onion
1/2	cup chopped green bell pepper
2	large chicken breasts, cooked and chopped
1	cup uncooked wild rice
1/2	cup blanched almonds
1	(4-ounce) can mushrooms
1	(8-ounce) can water chestnuts
41/2	cups water
2	envelopes dry chicken noodle soup mix
1/2	cup cooking sherry
1/2	(3-ounce) can French-fried onions

Brown the sausage in a skillet. Remove the sausage to a plate, reserving the drippings in the skillet. Cut the sausage into 1/2-inch pieces. Sauté the celery, onion and bell pepper in the reserved drippings until tender. Combine the sausage, chicken, sautéed vegetables, rice, almonds, mushrooms and water chestnuts in a large bowl and mix well. Bring the water to a boil in a saucepan. Add the soup mix and stir until dissolved. Pour over the rice mixture. Chill, covered, for 1 to 12 hours.

Preheat the oven to 350 degrees. Spoon the rice mixture into a baking dish. Bake for 11/2 to 2 hours. Sprinkle with the sherry. Top with the French-fried onions.

Serves 8 to 10

MUSHROOM BARLEY

13/4	cups pearl barley
1	cup chopped onion
1/2	cup (1 stick) butter
1	quart (4 cups) chicken broth
8	to 10 mushrooms
2	tablespoons soy sauce
1/2	teaspoon salt
	Pepper to taste

Sauté the barley and onion in the butter in a large skillet until the onion is translucent. Add the broth, mushrooms, soy sauce, salt and pepper and mix well. Simmer for 1 hour or until the liquid is absorbed. Do not overcook.

Note: To bake, preheat the oven to 325 degrees. Spoon the barley mixture into a baking dish. Bake, uncovered, for 2 hours. Do not use instant barley.

Serves 10

CHEESE HOMINY GRITS

5 1/2 cups water
3/4 cup light whipping cream
1/2 cup (1 stick) butter
1 tablespoon seasoned salt
3/4 teaspoon Tabasco sauce,
  or to taste
1 1/2 cups hominy grits
16 ounces sharp Cheddar
  cheese, shredded
3 eggs, lightly beaten

Bring the water, cream, butter, seasoned salt and Tabasco sauce to a simmer in a large saucepan. Whisk in the grits gradually. Cook at a very low simmer for 12 to 15 minutes or until most of the liquid is absorbed and the grits are creamy and thick, stirring frequently. Remove from the heat. Add the cheese and stir until melted. Cool for a few minutes. Adjust the seasonings to taste. Stir in the eggs. Preheat the oven to 350 degrees. Spoon the grits mixture into a greased 9×13-inch baking dish. Bake for 45 to 60 minutes or until the center is set. Preheat the broiler. Broil until light brown on top. Let stand for 10 minutes before serving.

Serves 8 to 10

SAUSAGE STUFFING

1 pound bulk pork sausage
2 onions, chopped
1/2 cup chopped celery
1/4 cup (1/2 stick) butter, melted
2 cups lightly toasted
  bread cubes
7 ounces chicken stock
1 1/2 teaspoons sage, or to taste
Salt and pepper to taste

Preheat the oven to 350 degrees. Cook the sausage in a large skillet just until the sausage begins to brown, stirring until crumbly. Add the onions and celery. Cook until the vegetables are tender and the sausage is brown, stirring frequently; drain. Place in a large bowl. Add the butter, bread, stock and sage and mix well. Season with salt and pepper. Adjust the sage to taste. Spoon into a greased 7×11-inch baking pan. Bake for 45 to 50 minutes or until brown on top.

Serves 12

SAUTÉED BRUSSELS SPROUTS WITH HAZELNUTS

1   handful of hazelnuts, chopped
2   cups brussels sprouts, rinsed
1   tablespoon butter
1   tablespoon olive oil
3   tablespoons apple
     cider vinegar

Photograph at left.

Preheat the oven to 350 degrees. Place the hazelnuts on a baking sheet. Bake for 10 minutes or until roasted. Cut the bottoms off the brussels sprouts. Chiffonade the heads of the brussels sprouts. Heat the butter and olive oil in a saucepan over medium heat. Add the brussels sprouts. Sauté over medium heat for 10 minutes or to the desired degree of crispness, adding the roasted hazelnuts during the last few minutes of sautéing. Add the vinegar just before serving.

Serves 4

FESTIVE HOLIDAY GREEN BEANS

3   pounds haricot verts,
     trimmed
8   ounces sliced bacon
1/2   cup chopped shallots
2   garlic cloves, chopped
1/4   cup sherry wine vinegar
3   tablespoons Dijon mustard
1   teaspoon dry mustard
1/3   cup olive oil
4   ounces crumbled goat cheese
1/2   cup fresh pomegranate seeds
     Salt and pepper to taste

Cook the green beans in water in a saucepan until tender-crisp; drain. Cook the bacon in a skillet until brown and crisp. Remove the bacon to paper towels to drain, reserving the drippings in the skillet. Crumble the bacon. Sauté the shallots and garlic in the reserved bacon drippings until soft. Add the vinegar, Dijon mustard and dry mustard. Whisk in the olive oil gradually. Add the green beans and toss to coat. Place in a serving bowl. Sprinkle with the goat cheese, bacon, pomegranate seeds, salt and pepper. Serve immediately.

Serves 6

This year, leave the traditional green bean casserole at home. Colorful and easy to prepare, this dish will make anyone look like a culinary genius.

BARBECUED BEANS

3 slices bacon, chopped
1 large onion, chopped
1 (15-ounce) can green beans
1 (15-ounce) can red
   kidney beans
1 (15-ounce) can pork
   and beans
1 (15-ounce) can yellow beans
1 1/2 cups packed brown sugar
1 cup ketchup
3 tablespoons white vinegar
1 tablespoon
   Worcestershire sauce
1 tablespoon dry mustard
1 teaspoon salt

Preheat the oven to 325 degrees. Sauté the bacon and onion in a skillet until the onion is brown and the bacon is crisp; drain. Combine with the beans in a large bowl. Add the brown sugar, ketchup, vinegar, Worcestershire sauce, dry mustard and salt and mix well. Spoon into a large baking pan. Bake for 30 minutes or to the desired consistency.

Serves 10

BROCCOLINI

3 bunches broccolini
   Salt to taste
2 tablespoons olive oil
3 garlic cloves, minced
3 oil-pack anchovies
1/4 teaspoon red pepper flakes
   Black pepper to taste
   Juice of 1/2 lemon
1/2 cup currants
1/2 cup toasted coarse
   bread crumbs

Blanch the broccolini in boiling salted water in a large saucepan for 3 minutes. Plunge immediately into ice water to stop the cooking process; drain.

Heat the olive oil in a large skillet over medium-high heat. Add the garlic, anchovies, red pepper flakes, salt and black pepper. Sauté for 3 minutes or until fragrant, mashing the anchovies with a wooden spoon. Add the lemon juice and currants. Sauté for 1 minute. Add the broccolini and toss to mix. Cook for 5 minutes or until the broccolini is tender-crisp, stirring occasionally. Season with salt and black pepper. Spoon onto a serving platter. Sprinkle with the bread crumbs.

Serves 4

Marinated Beets

Ginger Marinade

- 1 teaspoon grated fresh ginger
- 1 garlic clove, minced
- 1 tablespoon toasted sesame oil
- 1 tablespoon canola oil
- 1 tablespoon rice wine vinegar or cider vinegar
- 1 tablespoon tamari

For the ginger marinade, combine the ginger, garlic, sesame oil, canola oil, vinegar and tamari in a bowl and mix well.

Balsamic Marinade

- 2 garlic cloves, minced
- 2 tablespoons olive oil
- 1 tablespoon balsamic vinegar
- 1/4 cup chopped parsley
- Salt and pepper to taste

For the balsamic marinade, combine the garlic, olive oil, vinegar, parsley, salt and pepper in a bowl and mix well.

Beets

- 5 large beets

For the beets, scrub the beets and cut off the tops and bottoms. Cut the beets into halves and place in a saucepan. Cover with water. Bring to a boil. Reduce the heat and simmer for 30 minutes or until the beets are soft; drain. Rinse in cold water. Peel the beets. Let stand until cool. Cut the beets into thin slices. Serve with the desired marinade.

Serves 2 to 4

GREENS WITH CANNELLINI BEANS AND WINTER SQUASH

2 small delicata winter squash

3 tablespoons olive oil

I large onion, chopped

3 garlic cloves, chopped

I (15-ounce) can
   cannellini beans

1/2 cup water or stock

   Chopped fresh sage to taste

   Chopped fresh rosemary
   to taste

   Salt and pepper to taste

I large bunch kale or collard
   greens, rinsed and torn into
   bite-size pieces

Preheat the oven to 350 degrees. Cut the squash into halves and remove the seeds. Place the squash cut side down in an oiled baking pan, add some water to reduce sticking. Bake until soft.

Heat the olive oil in a large heavy saucepan with a tight-fitting lid. Add the onion. Cook for several minutes or until soft. Add the garlic, undrained beans, 1/2 cup water, sage, rosemary, salt and pepper and mix well. Cook, tightly covered, for several minutes. Stir in the kale. Cook, tightly covered, over medium heat until the kale is tender, stirring every couple of minutes. Remove from the heat.

Cut the unpeeled squash into bite-size pieces. Stir the squash gently into the kale mixture. Cook until heated through. Serve warm.

Serves 4 to 6

SAUTÉED KALE OR COLLARDS

1 bunch kale or collard greens
3 garlic cloves, minced
2 tablespoons olive oil
   Salt and pepper to taste
   Dash of balsamic vinegar
1/2 cup toasted pine nuts

Chop the kale into bite-size pieces. Sauté the garlic in the olive oil in a medium skillet. Stir in the kale. Cook, covered, for a few minutes or until the kale has softened but is still bright green. Stir in the salt, pepper, vinegar and pine nuts. Spoon into a serving dish.

Serves 4

ROASTED CARROTS AND SHALLOTS

2 pounds carrots, peeled
   and cut lengthwise
   into halves
8 ounces shallots,
   cut into halves
1 tablespoon chopped
   rosemary leaves
1 tablespoon olive oil
   Salt and pepper to taste

Preheat the oven to 450 degrees. Toss the carrots, shallots and rosemary with the olive oil on a rimmed baking sheet to coat. Sprinkle with salt and pepper. Roast for 10 to 12 minutes or until tender.

Serves 4

DUTCH OVEN POTATOES

6   cups thinly sliced potatoes
I   large onion, thinly sliced
3/4 cup (1 1/2 sticks) butter,
     chopped
I   cup water
I   tablespoon chili powder
2   teaspoons minced garlic
I   teaspoon garlic salt
    Salt and pepper to taste

Preheat the oven to 350 degrees. Combine the potatoes, onion, butter, water, chili powder, garlic and garlic salt in a Dutch oven and mix well. Bake for 45 minutes or until the potatoes are tender, stirring two or three times. Season with salt and pepper.

Serves 6

LEEK AND POTATO GRATIN

1 1/2 pounds leeks, sliced
2   tablespoons butter
5   potatoes, peeled and sliced
1 1/4 teaspoons salt
1/2 teaspoon pepper
I   cup whipping cream
1/2 cup chicken broth
3   garlic cloves, minced
I   bay leaf
1/2 teaspoon nutmeg
2   cups (8 ounces) grated
    Parmesan cheese

Preheat the oven to 400 degrees. Sauté the leeks in the butter in a skillet until tender. Toss the leeks with the potatoes, salt and pepper in a bowl to coat. Place in a greased 9×13-inch baking pan. Bake, covered with foil, for 40 minutes. Bring the cream, broth, garlic, bay leaf and nutmeg to a boil in a saucepan. Discard the bay leaf. Pour over the potato mixture and sprinkle with the cheese. Bake, uncovered, for 30 minutes.

Serves 6

CREAMY AU GRATIN POTATOES

1 1/2 pounds red potatoes
1/4 cup minced onion
      Salt and black pepper
      to taste
2 tablespoons butter
2 tablespoons all-purpose flour
2 cups milk
1 large garlic clove, minced
      Pinch of nutmeg
      Pinch of cayenne pepper
1 teaspoon salt
1 1/2 cups (6 ounces) shredded
      sharp white Cheddar cheese
1/2 cup (2 ounces) grated
      Parmesan cheese

Preheat the oven to 400 degrees. Scrub the potatoes. Cut the unpeeled potatoes into 1/4-inch slices. Layer one-half of the potatoes in a buttered 1 1/2-quart baking dish. Sprinkle with the onion. Top with the remaining potatoes. Sprinkle with salt and black pepper to taste.

Melt the butter in a medium saucepan over medium-high heat. Whisk in the flour for 1 minute. Stir in the milk, garlic, nutmeg, cayenne pepper and 1 teaspoon salt. Cook for 2 to 3 minutes or until the sauce thickens and coats the back of a spoon. Stir in the Cheddar cheese and Parmesan cheese. Cook for 30 to 60 seconds or until the cheese melts, stirring constantly. Pour over the potato layers. Bake, covered with foil, for 1 hour and 35 minutes, removing the foil during the last 20 minutes of baking. Let stand for 5 minutes to thicken before serving.

Serves 8

Potato Gratin with Smoked Gouda

3   pounds Yukon Gold potatoes,
     peeled and sliced
1   cup (4 ounces) shredded
     smoked Gouda cheese
2   tablespoons butter
5   garlic cloves, minced
1 1/2   cups whipping cream
1   teaspoon salt
1/2   teaspoon pepper

Preheat the oven to 350 degrees. Layer one-half of the potatoes, one-half of the cheese and then the remaining potatoes in a greased 9×13-inch baking dish. Melt the butter in a skillet. Add the garlic and sauté until golden brown. Pour over the layers. Mix the cream, salt and pepper in a bowl. Pour over the layers. Sprinkle with the remaining cheese. Bake for 1 hour and 25 minutes or until the cheese is golden brown.

Serves 8 to 10

This classic potato side can be modified by using Gruyère, Emmentaler, or sharp Cheddar. Other options include adding finely chopped ham, bacon, or green onions.

Potato Soufflé

3   potatoes, peeled and chopped
1   cup cottage cheese
1/2   cup (2 ounces) shredded
     white Cheddar cheese
2   tablespoons butter
1   egg yolk
     Salt to taste
1/8   teaspoon white pepper
1   egg white

Preheat the oven to 350 degrees. Boil the potatoes in water in a saucepan until tender; drain. Combine the potatoes, cottage cheese, Cheddar cheese, butter, egg yolk, salt and white pepper in a mixing bowl and beat well. Beat the egg white in a bowl until stiff peaks form. Fold into the potato mixture. Spoon into an 8×8-inch baking dish sprayed with nonstick cooking spray. Bake for 15 minutes. Serve immediately.

Serves 8

Indian-Style Potatoes (Aloo Subji)

3 large Idaho potatoes
3 tablespoons vegetable oil
1 teaspoon cumin seeds
1 bunch green onions, chopped
1 bunch cilantro, chopped
1 teaspoon turmeric
2 teaspoons coriander
1 to 2 teaspoons salt
1/2 teaspoon cayenne pepper
1 1/2 teaspoons garam masala
1 tablespoon lemon juice
Salt to taste

Scrub the potatoes. Place in a large saucepan and cover with water. Bring to a boil. Cook until tender. Drain and rinse in cold water to cool. Rub the skin off with your finger or with a small knife. Rinse the potatoes again. Cut into 1-inch pieces.

Heat the oil in a large skillet over medium-high heat. Add the cumin seeds. Cook until the cumin seeds begin to sizzle. Add the green onions. Cook for 2 to 3 minutes. Add the cilantro. Cook for 2 to 3 minutes. Add the turmeric, coriander, 1 to 2 teaspoons salt and the cayenne pepper. Add the potatoes and stir to coat with the spices. Reduce the heat to medium. Cook, covered, for 10 to 15 minutes or until the potatoes are soft and break apart easily with a fork, stirring occasionally. Increase the heat to high. Uncover and cook until the moisture has evaporated. Sprinkle with the garam masala and lemon juice. Cook over low heat for 5 minutes. Season with salt to taste. Garnish with additional cilantro.

Serves 6

BUTTERNUT SQUASH GRATIN

2 tablespoons olive oil

4 cups thinly sliced onions

4 sprigs of fresh thyme

2 tablespoons chopped
  fresh sage

1/2 teaspoon salt
  Pepper to taste

2 tablespoons olive oil

6 cups finely chopped
  butternut squash

1/2 cup all-purpose flour

2 tablespoons chopped
  fresh parsley
  Salt to taste

3/4 cup (3 ounces) grated fontina
  cheese or Gruyère cheese

1/2 cup plus 2 tablespoons
  warm milk

1 cup bread crumbs

Preheat the oven to 350 degrees. Heat 2 tablespoons olive oil in a skillet over medium heat. Add the onions, thyme and sage. Cook for 15 minutes or until the onions are caramelized, stirring frequently. Sprinkle with 1/2 teaspoon salt and pepper. Spread in a lightly oiled or buttered 2-quart gratin dish.

Return the skillet to medium heat and add 2 tablespoons olive oil. Dredge the squash in the flour to coat, shaking off the excess. Add to the hot olive oil. Sauté for 7 minutes or until the squash begins to brown on each side. Sprinkle with the parsley and salt and pepper to taste. Cook for 1 minute. Layer the squash mixture over the onions. Cover with the cheese. Pour the warm milk over the top. Bake, covered, for 25 minutes. Uncover and sprinkle with the bread crumbs. Bake for 25 minutes or until the top is brown and the liquid is absorbed.

Serves 6 to 8

Sweet Potato Casserole

2   (40-ounce) cans sweet
     potatoes, drained
2   eggs
1/2 cup (1 stick) butter, softened
11/2 teaspoons vanilla extract
1   cup granulated sugar
1/3 cup milk
1/2 cup packed brown sugar
1/4 cup all-purpose flour
21/2 teaspoons butter, softened
11/2 cups chopped pecans

Preheat the oven to 325 degrees. Place the sweet potatoes in a large baking dish. Combine the eggs, 1/2 cup butter, vanilla, granulated sugar and milk in a bowl and mix well. Pour over the sweet potatoes. Mix the brown sugar, flour, 21/2 teaspoons butter and the nuts in a bowl until crumbly. Sprinkle over the top. Bake for 35 to 45 minutes or until heated through.

Serves 8 to 10

Zucchini Fans

2 zucchini
2 tablespoons olive oil
  Salt and pepper to taste
1/3 cup chopped tomatoes
2 tablespoons chopped basil
1/4 cup (1 ounce) grated
  Parmesan cheese

Preheat the oven to 350 degrees. Line a small baking dish with foil and spray with nonstick cooking spray. Cut each zucchini lengthwise to 1/4 inch from the top four times. Place in the prepared baking dish and spread gently apart to form a fan. Brush with the olive oil, salt and pepper. Bake for 15 minutes or until tender. Remove from the oven. Preheat the broiler. Sprinkle the zucchini with the tomatoes, basil and cheese. Broil for 3 minutes or until the cheese is melted and the tomato and basil are heated through. Cut each zucchini fan into halves. Serve immediately.

Serves 4

Baked Basil Tomatoes

3 slices bread
4 ripe tomatoes
1 teaspoon sugar
1 teaspoon salt
1/4 teaspoon pepper
8 to 12 basil leaves
3 tablespoons butter, melted

Preheat the oven to 350 degrees. Cut the bread into small cubes. Place on a baking sheet. Bake for 20 minutes or until golden brown. Maintain the oven temperature. Cut the tomatoes into halves crosswise. Arrange the bottom halves cut side up in a greased 2-quart baking dish. Arrange the bread cubes around the tomato halves. Mix the sugar, salt and pepper in a small bowl. Sprinkle one-half of the sugar mixture over the tomato halves. Place two or three basil leaves on top of each tomato half. Replace the top halves of the tomatoes cut side down. Sprinkle with the remaining sugar mixture. Drizzle with the butter. Bake for 35 minutes.

Serves 4

ROASTED CHERRY TOMATOES

1 pound cherry tomatoes
2 tablespoons olive oil
2 garlic cloves, pressed
  Salt and freshly ground
  pepper to taste

Preheat the oven to 400 degrees. Toss the tomatoes with the olive oil, garlic, salt and pepper in a large bowl to coat. Place in a single layer on a rimmed baking sheet lined with foil or baking parchment. Bake for 25 to 30 minutes or until brown and caramelized.

Serves 4 to 6

Utah is one of the most ideal places for growing tomatoes. With summer temperatures hot, but not extreme, this climate yields an abundance of tomatoes, which are the heart of this simple recipe. Serve as a side dish or add to chicken, pasta, or fish. Make extra and freeze to enjoy the summertime flavor any time of year.

BAKED VEGETABLES WITH SOUR CREAM

2 cups chopped red
  bell peppers
2/3 cup chopped scallions
3 tablespoons butter
1 1/3 cups grated carrots
1/2 tablespoon minced parsley
4 yellow squash
1 1/2 teaspoons salt
1/2 teaspoon dried basil
1/2 teaspoon dried oregano
  Dash of pepper
1 cup sour cream
1 cup (4 ounces) grated
  Parmesan cheese

Preheat the oven to 350 degrees. Sauté the bell peppers and scallions in the butter in a skillet for 3 minutes. Add the carrots and parsley. Sauté for 3 minutes. Cut the squash into 1/2-inch pieces. Add to the skillet and sauté for 3 minutes. Sprinkle with the salt, basil, oregano and pepper. Remove from the heat. Add the sour cream and 2/3 cup of the cheese. Spoon into a 1 1/2-quart soufflé dish sprayed with nonstick cooking spray. Sprinkle with the remaining 1/3 cup cheese. Bake for 35 minutes.

Serves 8

PARKER HOUSE ROLLS

1 1/2 cups milk

1/4 cup (1/2 stick) butter

1/4 cup sugar

1 teaspoon salt

1 envelope dry yeast

1/4 cup warm water

1 egg, beaten

4 to 5 cups all-purpose flour

1/4 cup (1/2 stick) butter, melted

Scald the milk with 1/4 cup butter, the sugar and salt in a saucepan. Cool to lukewarm. Dissolve the yeast in the warm water in a glass cup. Pour the egg into the bowl of an electric stand mixer fitted with the paddle attachment. Add the yeast and milk mixture and stir to blend. Beat in 3 to 4 cups of the flour gradually at low speed. Continue to add the remaining flour gradually, beating to form a soft dough. Beat at high speed for 5 minutes.

Place the dough on a lightly floured surface. Knead for 6 to 10 minutes or until smooth and elastic. Shape into a ball and place in a greased bowl, turning to coat the surface. Let rise, covered with a towel, in a warm place for 1 1/2 hours or until doubled in bulk.

Place the dough on a lightly floured surface. Roll into a circle 1/3 inch thick. Cut out dough circles with a 3-inch round cutter. Dip the center of each dough circle in 1/4 cup melted butter and then fold in half. Place on a greased baking sheet with the sides touching. Brush the tops with the remaining melted butter. Let rise for 1 hour or until doubled in bulk. Preheat the oven to 375 degrees. Bake for 12 to 13 minutes or until light brown on top.

Makes 3 dozen

Inspired by First Lady of Utah Jeanette Herbert, this recipe is great for a large gathering. Serve the rolls warm from the oven with one of the many honey butter recipes on page 35.

ENDINGS

White Chocolate Tart with Honey-Roasted Peanut Crust 196 • Honey Pecan Tart 197

Apple Pie with Macadamia Nut Crumble 198 • Key Lime Pie 199

Fresh Peach Pie with Sunflower Seed Crust 200 • Peanut Butter Pie 201 • Apple Crisp 201

Fresh Apricot Turnovers 202 • Grilled Peaches 202 • Strawberries with Slide Ridge

Honey Wine Vinegar 203 • Raspberry Lemonade Sherbet 205 • Lemon Custard Ice Cream 205

Green Tea Ice Cream 206 • Vanilla Bean Ice Cream with Slide Ridge Honey Wine Vinegar 206

Raspberry Pecan Torte 207 • Caramel Banana Cake 208

Carrot Cake 209 • Chocolate Chip Bundt Cake 210 • Yogurt Chocolate Cake 211

Upside-Down German Chocolate Cake 212 • Rhubarb Cake 212

Cream Cheese Pound Cake 213 • Market Street Sabayon Sauce 213

Lehi Roller Mills Vanilla Cupcakes with Raspberry Cream Cheese Frosting 214

Oatmeal Butterscotch Bars 215 • Easy Brownies 215 • Salted Fudge Brownies 217

Chocolate Nut Meringues 217 • Cheesecake Bars 218

AvenueSweets Espresso Caramel Oat Bars 218 • Oatmeal Chocolate Chip Coconut Cookies 219

Favorite Oatmeal Cookies 219 • Caramel Shortbread 220

Chewy Brownie Cookies 220 • Molasses Spice Cookies 221 • Pecan Spice Cookies 221

Orange Chocolate Chip Cookies 222 • Buttermints 222 • Fudge 223

Graham Cracker Toffee Bark 223 • Amano Artisan Chocolate Pots de Crème 225

WHITE CHOCOLATE TART WITH HONEY-ROASTED PEANUT CRUST

Honey-Roasted Peanut Crust

- 3/4 cup honey-roasted peanuts
- 2 1/2 cups crushed graham crackers
- 1 teaspoon vanilla extract
- 5 tablespoons unsalted butter, melted

Filling

- 6 ounces white chocolate, chopped
- 3/4 cup heavy whipping cream, chilled

For the crust, preheat the oven to 350 degrees. Spray a tart pan with a removable bottom or a 9-inch pie plate with nonstick cooking spray. Chop the peanuts coarsely in a food processor. Reserve 1/4 cup of the peanuts. Add the graham crackers to the remaining peanuts and process to form coarse crumbs. Add the vanilla and butter and pulse until the crumbs are moistened. Press over the bottom and up the side of the prepared pan. Bake for 15 minutes or until golden brown. Remove to a wire rack to cool completely.

For the filling, melt the white chocolate in a double boiler, stirring frequently. Remove from the heat and stir until smooth. Cool slightly. Beat the whipping cream in a medium bowl until soft peaks form. Add the cooled melted white chocolate one-half at a time, beating for a few seconds after each addition to blend. Pour into the cooled tart shell. Chill for 4 hours or until the filling is set. Sprinkle the reserved 1/4 cup peanuts over the top just before serving.

Note: The tart may be prepared up to 2 days in advance and chilled until serving time.

Serves 8

Honey Pecan Tart

Tart Pastry

- 2 cups all-purpose flour
- 2 tablespoons sugar
- 1/2 teaspoon kosher salt
- 1 cup (2 sticks) butter, chilled and cut into 1/2-inch pieces
- 2 tablespoons ice water
- 2 tablespoons vanilla extract, chilled

For the pastry, mix the flour, sugar and kosher salt in a food processor. Add the butter. Pulse in three 30-second intervals or until only pea-size pieces of butter remain. Add a mixture of the ice water and vanilla, processing constantly until the mixture forms a ball. Wrap the pastry in plastic wrap and chill for 1 to 12 hours. Roll the pastry on a lightly floured surface into a circle 1/4 inch thick. Fit into a 10-inch tart pan, pressing firmly onto the bottom and up the side of the pan and being careful not to stretch the pastry. Prick all over the pastry with a fork. Cover with foil and press directly against the pastry. Freeze for 20 minutes. Preheat the oven to 375 degrees. Remove the foil. Bake the frozen pastry for 25 minutes or until golden brown. Maintain the oven temperature.

Filling

- 1 cup (2 sticks) butter
- 1 cup packed brown sugar
- 1/2 cup granulated sugar
- 1/3 cup honey
- 1/2 cup heavy cream
- 1 pound pecan halves

For the filling, melt the butter with the brown sugar, granulated sugar and the honey in a saucepan over low heat. Increase the heat to medium. Cook for 3 to 5 minutes, stirring frequently. Stir in the cream carefully as the mixture will bubble vigorously. Add the pecans and mix well. Pour just enough of the filling into the tart crust to fill just below the crust level. There may be some unused filling. Place the tart pan on a rimmed baking sheet and loosely cover the crust edge with foil. Bake for 15 minutes. Remove the foil and reduce the oven temperature to 350 degrees. Bake for 15 to 20 minutes or until the filling is set.

Serves 8 to 10

APPLE PIE WITH MACADAMIA NUT CRUMBLE

All-Purpose Pie Crust

1 1/4   cups all-purpose flour

1/2   teaspoon granulated sugar

1/4   teaspoon salt

1/2   cup (1 stick) unsalted butter, chilled and cut into pieces

3   to 4 tablespoons ice water

For the crust, whisk the flour, sugar and salt in a large bowl until mixed. Cut in the butter with a pastry blender or fork until crumbly. Add the ice water and mix to form a loose ball. Shape into a disk and wrap in plastic wrap. Chill for 1 hour or longer.

Macadamia Nut Crumble

1   cup all-purpose flour

1   cup packed brown sugar

Pinch of salt

7   tablespoons unsalted butter, chilled and cut into pieces

1/2   cup macadamia nuts, coarsely chopped and lightly toasted

For the crumble, mix the flour, brown sugar and salt in a bowl. Cut in the butter with a pastry blender or fork until crumbly. Reserve 1/4 cup of the crumble. Mix the nuts in the remaining crumble. Chill in the refrigerator.

Filling

1/4   cup packed brown sugar

1/4   teaspoon ground ginger

1/8   teaspoon coriander

1/8   teaspoon ground allspice

1   teaspoon vanilla extract

2   tablespoons lemon juice

Pinch of salt

3   pounds Golden Delicious apples or Granny Smith apples, peeled, cored and thinly sliced

1   tablespoon butter

For the filling, mix the brown sugar, ginger, coriander, allspice, vanilla, lemon juice and salt in a large bowl. Add the apples and the reserved 1/4 cup crumble and toss to mix. Let stand for 15 minutes, tossing occasionally.

Preheat the oven to 400 degrees. Unwrap the pastry disk and roll into a 13-inch circle on a lightly floured surface. Fit into a 9-inch pie plate, trimming and fluting the edge. Mound the apple filling in the center of the pastry and dot with 1 tablespoon butter. Top with the remaining crumble, patting down lightly. Bake for 1 hour or until the top is golden brown. Serve with whipped cream or ice cream.

Serves 8

KEY LIME PIE

Coconut Graham Cracker Crust

15 graham cracker squares,
   or 1 cup graham
   cracker crumbs

1/4 cup flaked coconut

1/4 cup pecans

1/4 cup sugar

5 tablespoons butter, melted

Filling

5 tablespoons butter, melted

1 (14-ounce) can sweetened
   condensed milk

4 egg yolks

1/2 cup Key lime juice
   Zest of 1 Key lime

2 cups heavy whipping
   cream, chilled

3 tablespoons sugar

1 teaspoon vanilla extract

For the crust, preheat the oven to 350 degrees. Process the graham crackers, coconut and pecans in a food processor to form a fine powder. Add the sugar and butter and mix well. Press over the bottom and up the side of an ungreased 9-inch pie plate. Bake for 10 minutes. Remove from the oven to cool completely.

For the filling, combine the condensed milk, egg yolks and lime juice in a mixing bowl and mix until smooth. Fold in the lime zest. Pour into the cooled crust. Bake for 25 minutes. Remove from the oven and cool for 15 minutes. Chill for 2 hours or longer until completed chilled.

Place a stainless steel mixing bowl in the freezer for 30 minutes. Pour the whipping cream into the prepared bowl and beat until soft peaks form. Add the sugar and vanilla and beat until firm peaks form. Spread over the top of the chilled pie. Garnish with toasted coconut and lime slices.

Serves 6

FRESH PEACH PIE WITH SUNFLOWER SEED CRUST

Sunflower Seed Pastry

3 cups spelt flour, kamut flour
   or whole wheat flour
1/2 teaspoon salt
1/3 cup sunflower seeds
1/4 cup canola oil
1/2 cups (about) water

Filling

10 large ripe peaches
2 tablespoons all-purpose flour
1 tablespoon lemon juice
3 tablespoons honey

For the pastry, blend the spelt flour, salt and sunflower seeds in a food processor until the consistency of cornmeal. Add the oil gradually, processing constantly. Add the water 1 tablespoon at a time until the pastry is lightly moist but not sticky. Divide the pastry into two equal portions. Roll each portion carefully on a lightly floured surface into a circle. Fit one circle into a 9-inch pie plate.

For the filling, preheat the oven to 400 degrees. Rinse the peaches well and pat dry. Cut the unpeeled peaches into slices. Combine the peaches, flour, lemon juice and honey in a bowl and toss to mix. Spoon into the pastry-lined pie plate. Top with the remaining pastry, fluting the edge and cutting vents. Bake for 10 minutes. Reduce the oven temperature to 300 degrees. Bake for 20 minutes longer or until the filling is bubbly and the crust is golden brown. Serve warm with vanilla ice cream.

Serves 6 to 8

Peanut Butter Pie

8 ounces cream cheese,
   softened
3/4 cup confectioners' sugar
1/2 cup creamy peanut butter
6 tablespoons milk
8 ounces frozen whipped
   topping, thawed
1 (9-inch) graham cracker
   pie shell
1/4 cup chopped peanuts

Beat the cream cheese in a mixing bowl until fluffy. Add the confectioners' sugar and peanut butter and mix well. Add the milk gradually, beating constantly. Fold in the whipped topping. Spoon into the pie shell. Sprinkle with the peanuts. Chill for 8 to 12 hours.

Serves 6 to 8

Apple Crisp

10 large Granny Smith apples
1 tablespoon ground cinnamon
1/4 teaspoon nutmeg
3 1/2 cups sugar
3 cups all-purpose flour
1 1/2 teaspoons baking powder
   Pinch of salt
3 eggs
3/4 cup (1 1/2 sticks) butter,
   melted

Preheat the oven to 350 degrees. Peel and core the apples. Cut into wedges and place in a large bowl. Add the cinnamon, nutmeg and 1/2 cup of the sugar and toss to coat. Mix the remaining 3 cups sugar, the flour, baking powder and salt in a bowl. Add the eggs and mix with your hands until crumbly. Layer the apple mixture in a 9×13-inch glass baking dish. Sprinkle with the crumbly topping. Drizzle the butter evenly over the top. Bake for 35 to 40 minutes or until bubbly. Serve with whipped cream or ice cream.

Serves 12

Fresh Apricot Turnovers

1 pound fresh apricots, sliced
1 tablespoon lemon juice
  Grated zest of 1 lemon
3/4 cup sugar
1/4 teaspoon nutmeg
  Salt to taste
1 tablespoon water
1 sheet puff pastry
1 egg
1 tablespoon water
  Sugar for sprinkling

Combine the apricots, lemon juice, lemon zest, sugar, nutmeg, salt and 1 tablespoon water in a heavy saucepan. Cook over medium heat for 25 minutes or until thickened, stirring occasionally. Cool to room temperature.

Preheat the oven to 400 degrees. Cut the pastry into 4- to 5-inch squares. Beat the egg with 1 tablespoon water. Spoon 2 to 3 tablespoons of the apricot mixture into the center of each pasty square. Brush the edges with the egg mixture to moisten. Fold the pastry diagonally over the filling to form a triangle and press the edges to seal. Place on a baking sheet. Brush with the remaining egg mixture and sprinkle with sugar. Bake for 20 to 25 minutes or until golden brown. Serve with vanilla ice cream.

Serves 6

Grilled Peaches

2 fresh ripe peaches
2 tablespoons brown sugar,
  or more to taste
2 teaspoons rum

Preheat the grill. Cut the peaches into halves and remove the pits. Place 1/2 tablespoon brown sugar in each peach center and drizzle with the rum. Place on the rack of the grill as it is cooling down. Grill for 10 minutes or until soft. Serve warm with vanilla ice cream or Greek yogurt and honey.

Serves 2 to 4

STRAWBERRIES WITH SLIDE RIDGE HONEY WINE VINEGAR

1 pint fresh strawberries, hulled

2 tablespoons Slide Ridge honey wine vinegar

1/4 cup heavy whipping cream, chilled

1 teaspoon confectioners' sugar

1/2 teaspoon vanilla extract

2 tablespoons chopped mint

Cut the strawberries into quarters or slices and place in a small bowl. Add the vinegar and toss to coat. Let stand at room temperature for 2 hours, stirring occasionally.

Beat the whipping cream in a mixing bowl until soft peaks form. Add the confectioners' sugar and vanilla and beat until firm peaks form.

Spoon the strawberry mixture into two small glasses and add a dollop of the whipped cream. Sprinkle with the mint.

Serves 2

What started as a childhood beekeeping hobby has grown into a full-fledged business—Slide Ridge Honey. The Honey Vinegar they produce is made from 100% pure, raw honey. Each batch of vinegar is unique in color and flavor, varying with the Utah mountain wildflowers in bloom.

RASPBERRY LEMONADE SHERBET

1 1/3 cups sugar

2 2/3 cups milk

1/3 cup cream

Zest and juice of
2 large lemons

1 tablespoon lemon extract

1 cup raspberries,
coarsely chopped

Photograph at left.

Mix the sugar, milk, cream, lemon zest, lemon juice and lemon extract in a nonreactive bowl. Chill for 8 to 12 hours. Freeze the raspberries in a freezer bag for 8 to 12 hours.

Pour the lemon mixture in an ice cream freezer container. Freeze using the manufacturer's directions, adding the raspberries 5 to 10 minutes before the end of the freezing process. Spoon into a freezer container and freeze until firm. Scoop 1/2 cup of the sherbet into each serving dish and garnish with additional fresh raspberries.

Serves 16

LEMON CUSTARD ICE CREAM

3/4 cup grated lemon zest

1 1/3 cups sugar

1 1/4 cups fresh lemon juice

6 egg yolks

1 1/2 cups cream

1 1/2 cups half-and-half

1/8 teaspoon salt

1 teaspoon lemon extract

Pulse the lemon zest and half the sugar in a food processor until mixed. Stir into the lemon juice in a microwave-safe bowl. Microwave on Medium-Low for 2 minutes, stirring at 30-second intervals. Let stand until cool.

Mix the egg yolks, 1 cup of the cream and 1 cup of the half-and-half in a large mixing bowl. Heat the remaining cream, half-and-half, sugar and the salt in a large saucepan until the mixture is steamy and the sugar is dissolved, stirring constantly. Whisk most of the hot mixture gradually into the egg yolk mixture. Add the egg yolk mixture to the remaining hot mixture, stirring constantly. Heat over low heat to 175 degrees on a candy thermometer. Strain into a large bowl and let stand until cool. Stir in the lemon extract and lemon juice mixture. Chill until ready to freeze. Pour into an ice cream freezer container. Freeze using the manufacturer's directions. Spoon into dessert dishes.

Serves 6 to 8

GREEN TEA ICE CREAM

1/2   vanilla bean

1 1/4   cups milk

2   egg yolks, beaten

1/4   cup castor sugar

1 1/4   cups heavy cream

1   teaspoon matcha (natural green tea powder)

Split the vanilla bean and scrape the seeds into a saucepan. Add the vanilla pod and milk. Bring to a gentle boil. Remove from the heat and let stand for 5 to 6 minutes. Discard the vanilla bean. Stir the egg yolks, sugar, cream and matcha into the milk. Cook over medium heat until thickened, stirring constantly. Remove from the heat and cool completely. Pour into an ice cream freezer container. Freeze using the manufacturer's directions. Spoon into dessert dishes.

Serves 6 to 8

VANILLA BEAN ICE CREAM WITH SLIDE RIDGE HONEY WINE VINEGAR

1/2   vanilla bean

4   cups half-and-half

1/2   cup Slide Ridge honey

6   egg yolks

     Slide Ridge honey

     wine vinegar

Split the vanilla bean and scrape out the seeds into a saucepan. Stir in the half-and-half and honey. Bring to a simmer over medium heat. Whisk the egg yolks in a small mixing bowl until smooth. Add 1 cup of the hot mixture gradually to the egg yolks, stirring constantly. Whisk the egg yolks into the remaining hot mixture in the saucepan. Bring to a simmer. Cook for 4 to 6 minutes or until the mixture coats the back of a spoon, stirring constantly. Pour into a glass bowl. Place plastic wrap directly on the surface of the mixture to prevent a skin from forming. Let stand to cool completely. Pour into an ice cream freezer container. Freeze using the manufacturer's directions. Spoon into dessert dishes and drizzle with vinegar.

Serves 6 to 8

Raspberry Pecan Torte

Torte

- 6 egg whites, at room temperature
- 2 teaspoons baking powder
- 2 teaspoons vanilla extract
- 2 cups sugar
- 1 cup pecans, chopped
- 1 cup crushed soda crackers
- 2 cups whipped cream

For the torte, preheat the oven to 350 degrees. Beat the egg whites in a mixing bowl until fluffy. Add the baking powder and vanilla and beat until soft peaks form. Add the sugar gradually, beating until stiff peaks form. Fold in the pecans and crackers. Spread in a greased 9×13-inch baking dish. Bake for 25 to 30 minutes or until golden brown. Remove from the oven and cool completely. Frost with the whipped cream. Chill, covered with foil, for 24 hours.

Raspberry Sauce

- 1 (4-ounce) package raspberry Danish Dessert pudding, pie filling and glaze mix
- 2 (16-ounce) packages frozen raspberries

For the raspberry sauce, prepare the glaze using the package directions for fruit sauce. Stir in the raspberries. Let stand until cool. Spoon over the torte and serve.

Serves 12

CARAMEL BANANA CAKE

Cake

1 1/2 cups all-purpose flour

1 teaspoon baking soda

3/4 cup sour cream

1 tablespoon milk

1/2 cup (1 stick) unsalted butter, softened

3/4 cup packed light brown sugar

2 medium eggs

3 ripe bananas, mashed

1 teaspoon vanilla extract

Caramel Icing

1/4 cup (1/2 stick) unsalted butter

1/2 cup packed light brown sugar

2 tablespoons sour cream

1 1/2 cups confectioners' sugar, sifted

1 to 3 tablespoons milk (optional)

For the cake, preheat the oven to 350 degrees. Sift the flour and baking soda together. Mix the sour cream and milk in a small bowl. Cream the butter and brown sugar in a large mixing bowl until light and fluffy. Beat in the eggs one at a time. Stir in the bananas. Add one-half of the flour mixture and mix until moistened. Add the sour cream mixture and mix well. Add the remaining flour mixture and vanilla and mix well. The batter will be slightly chunky. Pour into a greased 5×9-inch loaf pan. Bake for 50 to 60 minutes or until the cake tests done. Cool in the pan for 5 to 10 minutes. Invert onto a wire rack to cool completely.

For the icing, melt the butter and brown sugar in a medium saucepan over medium-low heat for 2 minutes, stirring constantly. Add the sour cream. Bring to a boil and then remove from the heat. Stir in the confectioners' sugar. If the icing is too thick, stir in the milk 1 tablespoon at a time until of the desired consistency. Spread over the cool cake.

Serves 8 to 12

Carrot Cake

Cake

2	cups all-purpose flour
2	cups sugar
1	tablespoon cinnamon
2	teaspoons baking powder
1	teaspoon salt
1 1/2	cups vegetable oil
2	teaspoons vanilla extract
4	eggs
3	cups grated carrots

For the cake, preheat the oven to 350 degrees. Mix the flour, sugar, cinnamon, baking powder and salt together in a large mixing bowl. Combine the oil, vanilla and eggs in a mixing bowl and mix well. Add to the flour mixture and mix well. Stir in the carrots. Spoon into a greased 9×13-inch cake pan or bundt pan. Bake for 45 to 55 minutes or until a wooden pick inserted in the center comes out clean. Cool in the pan for 10 minutes. Invert onto a wire rack to cool completely.

Orange Cream Cheese Frosting

8	ounces cream cheese, softened
1/2	cup (1 stick) unsalted butter, softened
1	tablespoon orange juice
2	teaspoons vanilla extract
4	cups confectioners' sugar

For the frosting, beat the cream cheese, butter, orange juice and vanilla in a mixing bowl until light and fluffy. Add the confectioners' sugar and beat until smooth. Spread over the cool cake.

Serves 12

CHOCOLATE CHIP BUNDT CAKE

Cake

- 1 (2-layer) package yellow cake mix
- 1 (4-ounce) package chocolate fudge instant pudding mix
- 1/2 cup sugar
- 3/4 cup vegetable oil
- 3/4 cup water
- 4 eggs
- 1 teaspoon vanilla extract
- 1 cup sour cream
- 1 cup (6 ounces) chocolate chips

For the cake, preheat the oven to 350 degrees. Combine the cake mix, pudding mix, sugar, oil and water in a mixing bowl and mix well. Add the eggs one at a time, stirring well after each addition. Stir in the vanilla and sour cream. Add the chocolate chips and mix well. Pour into a greased and floured bundt pan. Bake for 45 to 50 minutes or until the cake tests done. Cool in the pan for 10 minutes. Invert onto a wire rack to cool completely.

Chocolate Buttercream Frosting

- 1/4 cup (1/2 stick) butter, melted
- 2 cups confectioners' sugar
- 2 ounces unsweetened chocolate, melted
- 1 teaspoon vanilla extract
- 2 to 3 tablespoons milk or cream

For the frosting, combine the butter and 1/4 cup of the confectioners' sugar in a mixing bowl and mix well. Stir in the chocolate. Add the remaining 13/4 cups confectioners' sugar and mix well. Stir in the vanilla and enough of the milk to make a slightly runny consistency. Spoon over the cake.

Serves 10

Yogurt Chocolate Cake

Cake

2	cups all-purpose flour
2	cups sugar
1/4	cup baking cocoa
1	cup water
1/2	cup vegetable oil
1/2	cup (1 stick) butter
1	teaspoon baking soda
1/2	cup plain yogurt
2	medium eggs
1	teaspoon vanilla extract

For the cake, preheat the oven to 400 degrees. Mix the flour, sugar and baking cocoa together in a mixing bowl. Bring the water, oil and butter to a boil in a saucepan. Pour over the flour mixture and mix well. Dissolve the baking soda in the yogurt and stir into the batter. Add the eggs and vanilla and mix well. Pour into an ungreased 9×13-inch cake pan. Bake for 25 minutes.

Chocolate Frosting

1	(1-pound) package confectioners' sugar
1/4	cup baking cocoa
1	teaspoon vanilla extract
1/2	cup (1 stick) butter
1/3	cup milk

For the frosting, combine the confectioners' sugar, baking cocoa and vanilla in a mixing bowl and mix well. Heat the butter and milk in a saucepan until the butter melts. Pour over the sugar mixture and beat well. Spread over the warm cake.

Serves 10 to 12

Upside-Down German Chocolate Cake

1 1/2 cups shredded coconut

1 1/2 cups pecans

1 (2-layer) package German chocolate cake mix

1/2 cup (1 stick) butter

8 ounces cream cheese

1 (1-pound) package confectioners' sugar

Preheat the oven to 350 degrees. Spread the coconut and pecans in a greased and floured 9×13-inch cake pan. Prepare the cake mix using the package directions. Pour the batter over the coconut and pecans. Combine the butter and cream cheese in a microwave-safe bowl. Microwave on High until softened. Beat until creamy. Add the confectioners' sugar gradually, beating constantly until smooth. Carefully "lay" over the batter using a spatula, making the layer as even as possible. Bake for 45 minutes. Cut into squares to serve.

Serves 12 to 14

Rhubarb Cake

2 cups all-purpose flour

1 teaspoon baking soda

1 teaspoon salt

1/2 cup shortening

1 cup granulated sugar

1 egg

1 teaspoon vanilla extract

1/2 cup sour cream

1/2 cup buttermilk

3 cups (1/4- to 1/2-inch) rhubarb pieces

All-purpose flour for dusting

1/3 cup packed brown sugar

1 teaspoon cinnamon

Preheat the oven to 350 degrees. Sift 2 cups flour, the baking soda and salt together. Beat the shortening, granulated sugar, egg and vanilla in a mixing bowl until smooth. Add the flour mixture, sour cream and buttermilk and beat well. Dust the rhubarb with flour. Stir into the batter. Pour into a greased 9×13-inch cake pan. Sprinkle with a mixture of the brown sugar and cinnamon. Bake for 40 to 45 minutes or until the cake tests done.

Serves 8

CREAM CHEESE POUND CAKE

1 1/2 cups (3 sticks) butter,
   softened
8 ounces cream cheese,
   softened
3 cups sugar
   Dash of salt
1 1/2 teaspoons vanilla extract
6 eggs
3 cups sifted cake flour

Preheat the oven to 325 degrees. Beat the butter, cream cheese and sugar in a mixing bowl until fluffy. Beat in the salt and vanilla. Add the eggs one at a time, beating well after each addition. Stir in the cake flour. Spoon into a greased tube pan. Bake for 1 1/2 hours. Cool in the pan for 10 minutes. Cool completely on a wire rack.

Note: Make a Citrus Glaze of 1 cup superfine sugar and 6 tablespoons fresh lemon juice or orange juice. Pierce the top of the cake and slightly down the side with a cake tester. Pour one-half of the glaze gradually over the cake. Pierce additional holes in the cake. Pour the remaining glaze over the cake.

Serves 16

MARKET STREET SABAYON SAUCE

1 cup confectioners' sugar
1 cup dry white wine
1 cup triple sec
10 large egg yolks with
   chalazae (the thick cord-like
   strands of egg white attached
   to the egg yolk) removed

Cook the confectioners' sugar, wine, triple sec and egg yolks in a double boiler over medium heat until the consistency of a light custard, stirring constantly. Store in an airtight container in the refrigerator for up to 10 days.

Serves 8

The Market Street restaurants are a consistent favorite of Salt Lake City locals and visitors alike. They provide a dazzling array of fresh, high-quality seafood harvested from sustainable sources and flown in fresh daily. Market Street desserts are often purchased to-go when impressing guests is a priority. Serve this sauce over vanilla ice cream or as a topping for fresh summer berries. This delightful treat also pairs well with pound cake, meringue, or chocolate soufflé.

LEHI ROLLER MILLS VANILLA CUPCAKES WITH RASPBERRY CREAM CHEESE FROSTING

Raspberry Freezer Jam

- 2 pints fresh raspberries
- 4 cups superfine sugar
- 1 (3-ounce) package fruit pectin
- 3 tablespoons fresh lemon juice

Cupcakes

- 2 cups Lehi Roller Mills baking flour
- 1 1/2 cups sugar
- 1 tablespoon baking powder
- 1/2 teaspoon salt
- 1/2 cup (1 stick) butter, softened
- 1 cup 2% milk
- 1 1/4 teaspoons vanilla extract
- 4 egg whites

Raspberry Cream Cheese Frosting

- 1/2 cup (1 stick) butter, softened
- 8 ounces cream cheese, softened
- 1 teaspoon vanilla extract
- 2 to 3 cups confectioners' sugar
- 3 to 4 tablespoons Raspberry Freezer Jam
- 24 fresh raspberries

For the jam, crush the raspberries in a large bowl. Stir in the sugar until it dissolves. Blend the fruit pectin and lemon juice in a small bowl. Add to the berries and stir for 3 minutes or until thickened. Pour into three pint jars or six half-pint jars. Cover tightly and let stand at room temperature for 24 hours. Store in the freezer.

For the cupcakes, preheat the oven to 350 degrees. Mix the flour, sugar, baking powder and salt together in a medium bowl. Beat the butter, milk and vanilla in a mixing bowl until smooth and creamy. Add the flour mixture and mix well. Beat at low speed for 2 minutes, scraping the side of the bowl. Add the egg whites. Beat at high speed until fluffy. Fill paper-lined muffin cups half-full. Bake for 20 minutes or until a wooden pick inserted in the center comes out clean. Cool in the muffin pan for 10 minutes. Remove to wire racks to cool completely.

For the frosting, beat the butter and cream cheese at medium speed in a mixing bowl until very smooth. Mix in the vanilla. Add the confectioners' sugar gradually, beating constantly to the desired spreading consistency. Add the raspberry jam and mix well. Spread over the cupcakes. Top each with a fresh raspberry.

Makes 2 dozen

For more than 100 years, Lehi Roller Mills has been producing some of the finest quality baking flour in the country. Today it supplies flour to many large baking corporations and offers gourmet mixes for pancakes, breads, and cookies. Any light frosting will complement these simple vanilla cupcakes.

Oatmeal Butterscotch Bars

2 cups all-purpose flour

1 teaspoon baking soda

1 teaspoon salt

1 cup (2 sticks) butter, softened

1 cup packed brown sugar

1 teaspoon vanilla extract

2 eggs

2 cups rolled oats

1 cup chopped walnuts

1 (12-ounce) package
    butterscotch chips

Preheat the oven to 350 degrees. Mix the flour, baking soda and salt together. Beat the butter and brown sugar in a mixing bowl until fluffy. Add the vanilla and mix well. Beat in the eggs one at a time. Add the flour mixture and mix well. Stir in the oats and walnuts. Spread in a greased 9×13-inch baking pan. Sprinkle with the butterscotch chips. Bake for 3 minutes. Remove from the oven and swirl with a knife to marbleize. Bake for 15 minutes longer. Remove from the oven to cool. Cut into bars.

Makes about 2 dozen

Easy Brownies

1 cup plus 2 tablespoons
    canola oil

6 tablespoons baking cocoa

2 1/4 cups granulated sugar

5 eggs

2 cups all-purpose flour

1 teaspoon salt

2 teaspoons vanilla extract

1 cup (6 ounces) semisweet
    chocolate chips
    Confectioners' sugar

Preheat the oven to 350 degrees. Grease a 9×13-inch baking pan with butter and dust with baking cocoa. Combine the oil, baking cocoa, granulated sugar and eggs in a mixing bowl and beat at medium speed until well mixed. Add the flour, salt and vanilla and beat at low speed until blended. Fold in the chocolate chips. Spoon into the prepared pan. Bake for 25 to 30 minutes or until the edges begin to pull away from the sides of the pan. Sprinkle with confectioners' sugar while still hot. Cut into squares.

Makes about 2 dozen

SALTED FUDGE BROWNIES

3/4 cup (1 1/2 sticks)
   unsalted butter
2 ounces unsweetened
   chocolate, finely chopped
1 cup (6 ounces) semisweet
   chocolate chips
1/4 cup baking cocoa
2 cups sugar
3 eggs
1 1/2 teaspoons vanilla extract
1 cup all-purpose flour
1/2 teaspoon sea salt

Photograph at left.

Preheat the oven to 350 degrees. Melt the butter, chocolate and chocolate chips in a large saucepan over very low heat, stirring occasionally. Remove from the heat. Whisk in the baking cocoa, sugar, eggs and vanilla in the order listed. Whisk in the flour one-third at a time. Pour into a buttered 9×9-inch baking pan, smoothing the surface. Sprinkle the sea salt evenly over the top and swirl with a knife into the batter. Bake for 30 to 35 minutes or until the edges pull away from the sides of the pan and a wooden pick inserted into the center comes out with a little batter. Cool in the pan at room temperature for 1 to 2 hours or until firm.

Makes 16

CHOCOLATE NUT MERINGUES

4 egg whites, at room
   temperature
1/4 teaspoon salt
1/4 teaspoon cream of tartar
2 teaspoons vanilla extract
1 1/2 cups sugar
1/2 cup walnuts or pecans,
   chopped
1 cup (6 ounces)
   chocolate chips

Photograph at left.

Preheat the oven to 300 degrees. Beat the egg whites, salt, cream of tartar and vanilla at high speed in a mixing bowl until soft peaks form. Add the sugar gradually, beating until stiff peaks form. Stir in the walnuts and chocolate chips. Drop by spoonfuls onto a cookie sheet lined with baking parchment. Bake for 25 minutes or until firm to the touch, but not too brown. Cool on a wire rack.

Makes 2 dozen

CHEESECAKE BARS

1/3　cup butter
1/3　cup sugar
　1　cup sifted all-purpose flour
1/2　cup chopped walnuts
　8　ounces cream cheese,
　　　softened
1/4　cup sugar
　1　egg, beaten
　2　tablespoons milk
　1　tablespoon lemon juice
1/2　teaspoon vanilla extract

Preheat the oven to 350 degrees. Cream the butter and 1/3 cup sugar in a mixing bowl until light. Add the flour and walnuts and mix until crumbly. Reserve 1 cup of the crumb mixture. Press the remaining in a greased 8×8-inch baking pan. Beat the cream cheese and 1/4 cup sugar in a mixing bowl until smooth and creamy. Add the egg, milk, lemon juice and vanilla and beat well. Spread evenly over the crumb layer. Sprinkle with the reserved crumb mixture. Bake for 25 to 30 minutes or until set. Cool in the pan on a wire rack. Cut into bars and store in the refrigerator.

Makes 16

AVENUESWEETS ESPRESSO CARAMEL OAT BARS

11/2　cups all-purpose flour
11/2　cups old-fashioned oats
11/2　cups packed brown sugar
1/2　teaspoon baking soda
3/4　cup (11/2 sticks) unsalted
　　　butter, cut into pieces
　2　cups (12 ounces) dark
　　　chocolate chips or
　　　cinnamon chips
1/2　cup whipping cream
14　ounces AvenueSweets
　　　espresso caramels or
　　　pecan caramels

Preheat the oven to 350 degrees. Process the flour, oats, brown sugar and baking soda in a food processor until mixed. Add the butter and pulse until crumbly. Reserve 2 cups of the crumb mixture. Press the remaining in a greased 7×11-inch glass baking dish. Sprinkle with the chocolate chips. Bring the cream to a simmer in a saucepan. Add the caramels. Cook until smooth, stirring constantly. Pour over the crumb mixture. Sprinkle with the reserved crumb mixture. Bake for 15 minutes or until the edges are golden brown. Cool for 30 minutes. Chill for 3 hours or until set. Cut into bars.

Makes 2 dozen

———

AvenueSweets' handcrafted gourmet caramels are made the old-fashioned way—slow cooked in copper kettles—with locally produced Grade A butter, fresh whole cream, and the highest quality nuts. It is here that Old World European confection meets New World flavors, right in the heart of Utah.

———

OATMEAL CHOCOLATE CHIP COCONUT COOKIES

1	cup (2 sticks) butter, softened
2	cups packed brown sugar
2	eggs
1 1/2	teaspoons vanilla extract
1 1/2	cups all-purpose flour
1	teaspoon baking soda
1	teaspoon salt
3	cups rolled oats
2	cups (12 ounces) semisweet chocolate chips
1/2	cup flaked coconut

Preheat the oven to 350 degrees. Cream the butter and brown sugar in a mixing bowl until light and fluffy. Add the eggs and vanilla and beat well. Add the flour, baking soda, salt and oats and mix well. Stir in the chocolate chips and coconut. Drop by heaping tablespoonfuls onto a cookie sheet. Bake for 12 to 15 minutes or until light golden brown. Do not overbake. The cookies should still be slightly soft. Cool on the cookie sheet for 2 minutes. Remove to a wire rack to cool completely.

Makes 3 dozen

Photograph on page 216.

FAVORITE OATMEAL COOKIES

1	cup light brown sugar
1	cup (2 sticks) butter, softened
2	medium eggs
1	teaspoon vanilla extract
1 1/4	cups all-purpose flour
1	teaspoon baking soda
1	teaspoon salt
1	tablespoon cinnamon
1	teaspoon ground cloves
1	teaspoon ginger
3	cups rolled oats

Preheat the oven to 350 degrees. Combine the brown sugar, butter, eggs and vanilla in a mixing bowl and beat well. Add the flour, baking soda, salt, cinnamon, cloves, ginger and oats and mix well. Drop by tablespoonfuls onto a cookie sheet. Bake for 12 to 15 minutes or until golden brown. Cool on a wire rack.

Makes 3 dozen

Caramel Shortbread

1 1/2 cups all-purpose flour
1/4 cup granulated sugar
1 cup (2 sticks) unsalted butter
1/4 cup packed brown sugar
1 (14-ounce) can sweetened condensed milk
1 cup (6 ounces) chocolate chips, melted

Preheat the oven to 325 degrees. Mix the flour and granulated sugar in a bowl. Cut in 1/2 cup of the butter until the mixture resembles bread crumbs. Press over the bottom of a baking pan. Bake for 30 minutes or until light brown. Remove from the oven to cool. Melt the remaining 1/2 cup butter with the brown sugar in a saucepan. Stir in the condensed milk. Bring to a boil. Boil for 1 minute or until the color of light caramel. Pour over the shortbread. Let stand until cool. Spread the melted chocolate over the caramel. Let stand until set. Cut into bars.

Makes 16

Chewy Brownie Cookies

1 cup all-purpose flour
1/2 cup baking cocoa
1/4 teaspoon baking soda
1/2 teaspoon salt
1/3 cup shortening
1/3 cup butter, softened
1 1/2 cups packed brown sugar
1 tablespoon water
1 teaspoon vanilla extract
2 eggs
2 cups (12 ounces) semisweet chocolate chips

Preheat the oven to 375 degrees. Mix the flour, baking cocoa, baking soda and salt together. Beat the shortening, butter, brown sugar, water and vanilla in a mixing bowl until blended. Add the eggs and beat well. Beat in the flour mixture. Stir in the chocolate chips. Drop by tablespoonfuls onto a cookie sheet. Bake for 7 minutes. Cool on a wire rack.

Makes 2 dozen

MOLASSES SPICE COOKIES

2 cups all-purpose flour

2 teaspoons baking soda

1 1/2 teaspoons ginger

1/4 teaspoon ground cloves

1 teaspoon cinnamon

3/4 cup shortening

1 cup sugar

1 egg

1/4 cup dark molasses

1/3 cup sugar

Preheat the oven to 350 degrees. Sift the flour, baking soda, ginger, cloves and cinnamon together. Cream the shortening, 1 cup sugar and the egg in a mixing bowl. Add the molasses and mix well. Beat in the flour mixture until smooth. Shape into small balls and roll in 1/3 cup sugar. Place on a greased cookie sheet. Bake for 10 to 12 minutes or until firm. Cool on a wire rack.

Makes 2 dozen

Photograph on page 216.

PECAN SPICE COOKIES

3 1/4 cups all-purpose flour

2 teaspoons baking powder

1 teaspoon salt

1 1/2 teaspoons cinnamon

1 teaspoon nutmeg

1/4 teaspoon ground cloves

1/4 teaspoon ground allspice

1/2 cup shortening

1/2 cup (1 stick) butter, softened

2 cups packed brown sugar

1 teaspoon vanilla extract

2 eggs

1/3 cup sour cream

2 cups chopped pecans

1 cup (6 ounces) chocolate chips (optional)

Preheat the oven to 350 degrees. Mix the flour, baking powder, salt, cinnamon, nutmeg, cloves and allspice together. Cream the shortening, butter and brown sugar in a mixing bowl until light and fluffy. Add the vanilla, eggs and sour cream and mix well. Beat in the flour mixture. Stir in the pecans and chocolate chips. Drop by spoonfuls onto a greased cookie sheet. Bake for 14 minutes. Cool on a wire rack.

Makes 5 dozen

ORANGE CHOCOLATE CHIP COOKIES

2 1/4 cups all-purpose flour

1/2 teaspoon salt

1 cup (2 sticks) unsalted butter, softened

3 ounces cream cheese, softened

1 cup granulated sugar

1 teaspoon orange extract

2 medium eggs

1 teaspoon grated orange zest

1 cup (6 ounces) miniature semisweet chocolate chips

2 cups confectioners' sugar

3 ounces cream cheese, softened

1 teaspoon grated orange zest

2 to 3 teaspoons fresh orange juice

Preheat the oven to 350 degrees. Mix the flour and salt together. Beat the butter, 3 ounces cream cheese and the granulated sugar in a mixing bowl until light and fluffy. Add the orange extract and mix well. Beat in the eggs one at a time. Add the flour mixture and beat well. Stir in 1 teaspoon orange zest and the chocolate chips. Drop by tablespoonfuls onto a cookie sheet lined with baking parchment or a silicone sheet. Bake for 14 minutes. Cool on a wire rack.

Combine the confectioners' sugar, 3 ounces cream cheese and 1 teaspoon orange zest in a mixing bowl and mix well. Beat in enough orange juice to make of a spreading consistency. Frost the cooled cookies.

Makes 2 dozen

BUTTERMINTS

1 (1-pound) package confectioners' sugar

2 tablespoons butter, softened

1/4 cup mashed cooked potatoes

1 teaspoon mint flavoring

1 to 2 teaspoons water

Mix the confectioners' sugar, butter, potatoes, mint flavoring and 1 teaspoon water in a bowl until the mixture forms a solid mass, adding the remaining water if needed for the mixture to come together. Knead on a work surface to form a smooth dough. Shape 1 teaspoon of the dough at a time into balls. Store in an airtight container in the refrigerator.

Note: Tint with food coloring for variety if desired.

Makes about 1 pound

FUDGE

2 1/4 cups sugar
1/4 cup (1/2 stick) butter
4 ounces marshmallow creme
1/4 teaspoon salt
1 cup evaporated milk
1 teaspoon vanilla extract
1 cup (6 ounces) semisweet chocolate chips
1/3 cup dark chocolate chips
1 cup chopped nuts (optional)

Mix the sugar, butter, marshmallow creme, salt and evaporated milk in a heavy 2-quart saucepan. Bring just to a boil over medium heat, stirring constantly. Boil for 7 minutes, stirring constantly. Remove from the heat. Stir in the vanilla and chocolate chips until melted. Stir in the nuts. Spread in a buttered 8×8-inch pan. Let stand until cool. Cut into squares.

Note: For Layered Butterscotch Fudge, make another batch of the fudge, substituting butterscotch chips for the chocolate chips. Pour over the chocolate fudge and let stand until cool. Cut into squares.

Serves 24

GRAHAM CRACKER TOFFEE BARK

1/2 (14-ounce) package whole graham crackers
1 cup (2 sticks) unsalted butter
3/4 cup packed brown sugar
2 cups (12 ounces) chocolate chips
3/4 cup chopped almonds

This effortless dessert is sure to become a family favorite. Sprinkle with chocolate, butterscotch, mint, or peanut butter chips. Add chopped nuts or candy bars to personalize the bark for any occasion.

Preheat the oven to 350 degrees. Line a 10×15-inch rimmed baking sheet with foil and spray with nonstick cooking spray. Arrange the graham crackers with sides touching in the prepared pan, breaking to fit as needed. Melt the butter and brown sugar in a saucepan over medium heat, stirring constantly. Bring to a boil. Reduce the heat and simmer for 5 minutes, stirring frequently. Pour over the graham crackers to cover completely. Bake for 8 to 10 minutes, watching carefully to prevent burning. Remove from the oven. Let cool until the brown sugar mixture quits bubbling. Sprinkle the chocolate chips evenly over the top. Let stand for 2 to 3 minutes or until softened. Spread the chocolate evenly over the surface. Sprinkle with the almonds. Cool to room temperature, then chill in the refrigerator. Remove the foil and break the toffee bark into pieces. Place in a covered container and store in the refrigerator.

Serves 4

Amano Artisan Chocolate Pots de Crème

1 1/2 cups milk

1 cup heavy cream

1/2 cup sugar

1 vanilla bean, split and scraped

6 medium egg yolks

12 ounces Amano Artisan Guayas chocolate, chopped

Combine the milk, cream and sugar in a medium saucepan. Add the vanilla bean seeds and pod. Bring to a boil over medium heat. Remove from the heat. Whisk the eggs yolks in a bowl. Whisk one-third of the hot mixture into the beaten egg yolks. Whisk the egg yolks into the remaining hot mixture. Return to medium heat. Cook for 15 to 20 seconds or until slightly thickened, whisking constantly. Do not allow to boil. Remove from the heat. Add the chocolate to the hot mixture, pushing down to submerge. Let stand for 1 to 2 minutes or until the chocolate melts. Whisk until smooth. Strain through a fine wire mesh strainer, discarding the solids. Pour into ramekins or pot de crème cups. Chill for several hours or until set. Serve alone or with fresh berries, a dollop of whipped cream and a crisp cookie.

Serves 8 to 10

Pots de Crème are an impressive finish to any meal, yet are deceptively easy to prepare. When made with Amano Guayas Chocolate, this recipe offers a complex combination of fruity, floral, and spicy notes. Recognized as one of the best chocolatiers in the world, Utah-based Amano Chocolates uses only the freshest and highest quality ingredients.

Partnerships

The Junior League of Salt Lake City, Inc., has partnered
with the following organizations to promote the local food movement
that is becoming an increasingly important part of our community.
We share a common philosophy of supporting our
local companies, farmers, and food artisans.

Edible Wasatch

www.ediblewasatch.com

Local First Utah

www.localfirst.org

Slow Food Utah

www.slowfoodutah.org

Utah's Own

www.utahsown.utah.gov

Professional Contributors

Amano Artisan Chocolate

AvenueSweets

Beehive Cheese Company

Bell Organic

Cuisine Unlimited

Gastronomy, Inc.

Goldener Hirsch Inn Restaurant

Hell's Backbone Grill

Lehi Roller Mills

Log Haven

Lori Tolbert Catering

Lugano

Marguerite Henderson

Mazza Middle Eastern Cuisine

Meditrina

Miller's Honey Company

Montage Deer Valley

Morgan Valley Lamb

Naked Fish Japanese Bistro

Norbest

The Orton Group

Pago

Pepperlane Products

Redmond Incorporated

RJ Peterson

Roberts Restaurant

Ruby Snap

The St. Regis at Deer Valley

Slide Ridge Honey

Squatters Pub Brewery

Taylor Natural Farms

The Tea Grotto

Tom Woodbury

Viking Cooking School at
Kimball Distributing

Contributors

Sally Alberts
Connie Anderson
Connie Andrade
Lucy Archer
Joan Armstrong
Sarah Armstrong
Sarah Atzet
Nici Baer
Janis Baker-Ferre
Ali Neese Barber
Daneta Daniel Bardsley
Paula Barnes
Lynn Williams Barnette
Haley Baronne
Anne Cameron Barrett
Kris Battleson
Kelley Beaudry
Zach Beaudry
Sara Becker
Susan Becker
Emily Beckmann
Kelly Beebe
Emily Bergeson
Eric Bergstrom
Marilyn Bergstrom
Tori Bergstrom
Alexandra Bernardi
Heather Bertotti
Tara Bevins
Joyce Bjork
Gerri Blair
Holly Bowen
Jane Bowles
Patricia Bradley
Casey Breton
Diane Breton
Gail Breton

Sally Brown
Anna Brozek
Cherrie Bryan
Cindy Burian
Gayle Butler
Kevin Butler
Norinne Callister
Natasha Carrera
Lori Carter
Lexi Casalino
Cheryl Casey
Brad Cassell
Mary Ann Cassell
Amy Christensen
Daralyn Christensen
Diane Christensen
Greg Christensen
Brooke Clark
Jennifer Clark
Mona Daniels Clark
Pamela Clawson
Cindy Collins
Cynthia Conner
Christina Cook
Allison Cornett
Ryan Crook
Elizabeth Crowder
Erica Dahl
Sarah Dallof
Diane Dalton
Betty Davis
Eddie Davis
Patricia Davis
Allison Dayton
Quanda DeGraffenreidt
Stacy DeQuina
Jean Dise

Terrell Dougan
E.B. Drinkaus
Barbara Reese Dugan
Alice DuRoss
Carly Elliott
Carol Elliott
Elaine Ellis
Karen Thomas Ellison
Martha Farney
Jolie Fazio
Carol Firmage
Marlise Fisher
Jen Foote
Norine Foote
Si Foster
Allene Fowler
Josie Franciose
Jen Fraser
Pam Fullmer
Debra Furlong
Melissa Gaffney
Annie Garavatti
Andrea Gardner
Josie Gay
Claire Gaylord
Shirley Gentges
Coreen Gililland
Jennifer Gilroy
Kim Goebel
Lisa Graham
Sarah Grant
Kay Greene
Beverly Greener
Missy Greis
Penny Grikscheit
Susan Grodner
Marianne McGregor Guelker

CONTRIBUTORS

Rose Guilbeau
Jana Hadany
Nicole Hale
Sabrina Haller
Catherine Hammond
Phyllis Hansen
Christina Heartly
Carol Hellmer
Tara Hellmer
Lori Hendry
Jeanette Herbert
Rebecca Hewitt
Jani Hicken
Amanda Hill
Annette Hodder
Amy Hogan
Brittany Holman
Julie Holt
Monica Hope
Pamela Howard
Peter Hugie
Gloria Hyland
Chanda Jenkins
Ann Jensen
Richard Jewkes
Daniela Jex
Jennifer Johnston
Jim Johnson
Agnes Jones
Cara Jones
Dana Jones
Jean Jones
Sue Jones
Sally Kate Joye
Joni Justice
Brent Kelsey
Jennifer Kelsey

Sally Kelsey
Samantha Kelsey
Alice Kemnitz
Brittney Kennedy
Natalie Kennedy
Paige Kirch
Linda Knippel
Bev Knox
Jennifer Kohler
Jeanne Konishi
Kristin Kraus
Numsiri Kunakemakorn
Kelly LaDue
Ronda Landa
Karin Landstrom
Rholinda Lange
Jamie Larsen
Joan Larsen
Ann Lassley
Nicole Ledford
Sherlyn Lewis
Sissy Lieberman
Carolyn Lindsay
Hollis Logue
Andrea Low
Lindsay Low
Jon Lund
Betty Lutz
Cynthia Lyman
Jan Lyons
Heidi Makowski
Marie Malone
Kelly Martin
Carrie Martinez
Jan Massimino
Olivia Massimino
Anne Maxfield

Lauren Muenzberg McBrier
Alex McClain
Laurel McClain
Fran McCommon
Vicki McGavin
Chrisanne McGee
Callaway McKay
Ginny McKay
Lauren McKay
Leanne McQuade
Courtney McVicker
Lauri Voelkel Meidell
Robin Mengis
Victoria Mertes
Loren Micalizio
Liz Michie
Sallee Middlekauff
Lisa Mietchen
Staci Mihalopoulos
Jill Miller
Mikala Miller
Cathie Mooers
Sara Mulholland
Bradyn Mulvey
Gayle Nabrotsky
Joanne Neal
Sara Neal
Diana Neese
Jeff Neese
Joy Neese
Tammi Neese
Gary Nicolayson
Ashley Nielson
Amy Noble
Sara Norinne
Flannery O'Connor
Donna Ooms

CONTRIBUTORS

Larry Orton
Meredith Orton
Ema Ostarceric
Jean Overfelt
Krissi Paczolt
Sarah Pallot
Chris Panos
Michele Paoletti-Schelp
Jami Pappas
Marion Payne
Denise Perkins
Jaymie Perry
Natalie Perry
Debbie Peters
Ann Peterson
R.J. Peterson
Melissa Phillips
Sandra Pickhardt
Karen Piotrowski
Jean Pirog
Cheryl Pitkin
Krista Powell
Ginny Radice
Angela Rathbun
Carrie Reilly
Chris Reilly
Kristine Rhodes-George
Michael Richey
Jennifer Rigby
Chris Riggle
Mary-Anne Roberts
Jill Robertson
Pat Robertson
Sydnie Robertson
Karena Rogers
Rebekah Rosenthal
Suzanne Rothberg

Becky Ruley
Ragana Russo
Penny Jensen Sandberg
Theresa Ryan-Shearman
Hadley Saber
Angela Sampinos
Pam Sanford
Margaret Sargent
Sara Sargent
Gage Saunders
Dana Schaffer
Steve Scheuerelle
Jamie Schwarzenbach
Julia Seiders
Lara Shackelford
Sue Sharma
Andy Shearman
Rebecca Sheeran
Diane Sheya
J.W. Shields
Michael Showers
Lynda Simmons
Shellie Simpson
Robert Smith
Sally Smith
Erin Sofianos
Kitch Somers
Carol Spencer
Elizabeth Spiker
Gary Springer
Alan Staker
Eileen Staley
Elizabeth Strasser
Heather Strasser
Maggie Strasser
Heather Svendsen
Celesta Tagliaferri

Kaati Tarr
Kathy Thompson
Marian Thompson
Marty Thompson
Eric Thorpe
Jan Thorpe
Lori Tolbert
Jamie Treend
Marjorie Tuckett
Gwenyth Turk
Katie Tyser
Jeff Unruh
Polly Unruh
Mike Vanden Berg
Allison Volk
Lezlie Wade
Merrill Wall
Sarah Waters
Julia Watkins
Laura Wayment
Jessica Weber
Barbara Weber-White
Elizabeth Weeks
Sandra Weese
Katie Welch
Tracy Wennerholm
Margo Weston
Melany White-Flory
Jenny Williams
Fred Wix
Lisa Woodbury
Judy Wright
Merilyn Wright
Cindy Yamada Thomas
Karen Zaninovich-Parker
Ann Zimmerman

INDEX

━━━

Accompaniments. *See also* Butters;
    Salsas; Sauces
    Buttermilk Syrup, 24
    Chef's Dressing, 163
    Cranberry Chutney, 63
    Raspberry Compote, 23
    Raspberry Freezer Jam, 214
    Utah's Own Arugula Pesto, 57
    Whipped Cream, 23

Almonds
    Almond Biscotti, 27
    Almond Honey Butter, 35
    Black Pepper Almonds, 59
    Graham Cracker Toffee Bark, 223
    Nutty Apricot Goat Cheese
        Chicken Salad, 83
    Nutty Honey Granola, 33
    Pago's Cinnamon Beets with Nut
        Crunch and Truffle Honey, 75
    Sweet and Nutty Quinoa, 173

Amano Artisan Chocolate
    Amano Artisan Chocolate
        Pots de Crème, 225

Appetizers. *See also* Dips; Salsas;
    Snacks; Spreads
    Apple Fontina Bites, 55
    Asian Meatballs with Soy Honey
        Ginger Sauce, 44
    Cheese-Stuffed Mushrooms, 50
    Cheesy Artichoke Cups, 53
    Chinese Chicken Wings, 46
    Corn Cakes with Peach
        Mustard Sauce, 56
    Deviled Eggs with Tarragon and
        Watercress, 50
    Fava Bean Crostini, 55
    Gorgonzola-Stuffed Dates, 51
    Marguerite Henderson's Grilled
        Herbed Shrimp, 49
    Mexican Won Tons, 53
    Party Turnovers, 58
    Polenta Pesto Squares, 57

Pot Stickers, 45
Sassy Shrimp, 46
Skewered Shrimp with
    Peanut Dipping Sauce, 47

Apple
    Apple Crisp, 201
    Apple Fontina Bites, 55
    Apple Pecan Streusel
        Muffins, 30
    Apple Pie with Macadamia Nut
        Crumble, 198
    Apple-Stuffed Pork Chops, 131
    Dried Cherry, Apple and Pecan Salad
        with Maple Dressing, 94
    Frisée Salad, 158
    Great Scott Salad, 95
    Holiday Cranberry Chutney with
        Brie Cheese, 63
    Moroccan Carrot and
        Sweet Potato Soup, 103
    Northwest Autumn Salad, 97
    Pacific Salmon with Roasted Red
        Pepper Beurre Pomme, 164

Artichokes
    Cheesy Artichoke Cups, 53
    Pesto Chicken with Penne, 147

Asparagus
    Couscous Salad, 85
    Quinoa Salad with Grilled Asparagus,
        Goat Cheese and Black Olive
        Vinaigrette, 88

AvenueSweets
    AvenueSweets Espresso Caramel
        Oat Bars, 218

Bacon
    Bacon, Leek and Cheddar Cheese
        Mini Quiches, 12
    Bacon Vinaigrette, 91
    Gorgonzola-Stuffed Dates, 51
    Great Scott Salad, 95

Roasted Jalapeño, Bacon and
    Potato Soup, 99

Banana
    Banana Pancakes, 24
    Caramel Banana Cake, 208
    Fresh Fruit Salad, 34

Beans
    Barbecued Beans, 180
    Black Bean and Goat Cheese
        Enchiladas, 167
    Fava Bean Crostini, 55
    Festive Holiday Green Beans, 179
    Fresh Chicken Soup, 110
    Greens with Cannellini Beans and
        Winter Squash, 182
    Mexican Pork, 134
    Mexican Won Tons, 53
    Quinoa and Black Bean Salad, 87
    Ribollita, 104
    Spicy White Chili, 109
    Tamale Pie, 126
    Turkey and Vegetable Chili, 106
    Turkey White Bean Chili, 107
    Vegetarian Tikka Masala, 169
    White Bean Hummus, 65

Beef. *See also* Ground Beef; Veal
    Baked Stuffed Flank Steak, 118
    Barbecued Brisket, 119
    Company Stroganoff, 121
    Grilled Tri-Tip Roast, 120
    Mongolian Beef with Bean Sprouts, 123
    Roasted Garlic Beef Stew, 124

Beehive Cheese Company
    Utah's Own Arugula Pesto, 57
    Utah's Own Promontory Cheddar
        Lamb Burger, 73

Beets
    Marinated Beets, 181
    Pago's Cinnamon Beets with Nut
        Crunch and Truffle Honey, 75

Beverages
Champagne Cosmopolitan, 43
Hot Cranberry Punch, 43
Margaritas, 39
Papaya Colada, 38
Phil Collins Drink, The, 40
Pimm's Treat with Homemade
    Lemonade, 41
Pink Grapefruit Sparkling Sangria, 38
Pomtini, 40
Raspberry Mojito, 39

Blackberry
Greek Yogurt, Honey and Poppy Seeds
    with Blackberries, 33

Blueberry
Blueberry Crumble Muffins, 31
Fresh Fruit Salad, 34
Naked Fish Kudamono Salad, 96

Blue Cheese
Arugula and Fig Salad with Blue Cheese
    and Bacon Vinaigrette, 91
Blue Cheese Chicken Wing Dip, 66
Corn, Cherry Tomato, Arugula and
    Blue Cheese Salad, 92
Gorgonzola-Stuffed Dates, 51

Bok Choy
Stir-Fried Bok Choy and Shiitake
    Mushrooms, 168

Breads. *See also* Muffins
Almond Biscotti, 27
Banana Pancakes, 24
Beer, Basil and Asiago Bread, 52
Chocolate Zucchini Bread, 27
Chunky Monkey Cinnamon
    Bread, 29
French Toast with Pecans, 21
Hazelnut Zucchini Bread, 28
Parker House Rolls, 193
Peach Scones, 26
Perfect Waffles, 25

Raspberry Pancakes, 23
Sage and Prosciutto Popovers, 51
Waffles Deluxe, 25
Walnut Shortcake Biscuits, 26

Breakfast/Brunch. *See also* Breads;
    Egg Dishes; Quiche
Banana Pancakes, 24
Chile Relleno Casserole, 19
Deviled Eggs with Tarragon and
    Watercress, 50
Egg Casserole, 16
French Toast with Pecans, 21
Greek Yogurt, Honey and Poppy Seeds
    with Blackberries, 33
Jalapeño Goat Cheese Frittata, 15
Nutty Honey Granola, 33
Perfect Waffles, 25
Potato, Eggs and Chorizo Tacos, 18
Raspberry Pancakes, 23
Salmon and Grits, 20
Shirred Pancetta and Arugula Eggs, 16
Sunday Eggs, 17
Waffles Deluxe, 25
Zucchini Sausage Squares, 19

Brie Cheese
Amaretto and Brie Cheese, 61
Holiday Cranberry Chutney with
    Brie Cheese, 63

Broccoli
Basil Chicken Pasta Salad, 78
Thai Chicken in Spicy Peanut Sauce, 149
Vegetable Quiche, 13

Broccolini
Broccolini, 180
Couscous Salad, 85

Brussels Sprouts
Provençal Spareribs with Roasted
    Potatoes and Brussels Sprouts, 133
Sautéed Brussels Sprouts with
    Hazelnuts, 179

Butters
Almond Honey Butter, 35
Bavarian Honey Butter, 35
Cinnamon Honey Butter, 35
Garlic Butter, 52
Lemon Honey Butter, 35
Miller's Basic Honey Butter, 35
Orange Honey Butter, 35
Spiced Honey Butter, 35

Cabbage
Fish Tacos, 165
Goldener Hirsch Inn's Duck Confit with
    Riesling Choucroute, 157
Pot Stickers, 45
Ribollita, 104

Cakes
Caramel Banana Cake, 208
Carrot Cake, 209
Chocolate Chip Bundt Cake, 210
Cream Cheese Pound Cake, 213
Lehi Roller Mills Vanilla Cupcakes with
    Raspberry Cream Cheese Frosting, 214
Rhubarb Cake, 212
Upside-Down German Chocolate
    Cake, 212
Yogurt Chocolate Cake, 211

Candies
Buttermints, 222
Fudge, 223
Graham Cracker Toffee Bark, 223

Carrots
Baked Vegetables with Sour Cream, 192
Carrot Cake, 209
Chicken and Wild Rice Soup, 112
Coconut Curry Cashew Quinoa, 172
Fresh Chicken Soup, 110
Moroccan Carrot and
    Sweet Potato Soup, 103
Pork Ragù, 135
Roasted Carrots and Shallots, 183
Roasted Garlic Beef Stew, 124

Sweet and Crunchy Salad, 98
Turkey Vegetable Meat Loaf, 151
Vegetable Quiche, 13

Cashews

Coconut Curry Cashew Quinoa, 172
Nutty Apricot Goat Cheese
    Chicken Salad, 83
White Pepper Cashews, 59

Cauliflower

Vegetable Quiche, 13

Cheddar Cheese

Bacon, Leek and Cheddar Cheese
    Mini Quiches, 12
Cheese Hominy Grits, 177
Utah's Own Promontory Cheddar
    Lamb Burger, 73

Cheese. *See also* Blue Cheese;
    Brie Cheese; Cheddar Cheese;
    Goat Cheese
Apple Fontina Bites, 55
Beer, Basil and Asiago Bread, 52
Camembert Cheese Crisps, 60
Cheese-Stuffed Mushrooms, 50
Cheesy Artichoke Cups, 53
Chile Relleno Casserole, 19
Orecchiette with Fresh
    Mozzarella Cheese, 169
Orzo Salad with Spinach and Feta, 86
Potato Gratin with Smoked Gouda, 186
Rustic Prosciutto and Provolone
    Sandwich, 73
Tilapia in a Parmesan Cheese Sauce, 166

Chicken

Asian Chicken Pasta Salad, 77
Basil Chicken Pasta Salad, 78
Blue Cheese Chicken Wing Dip, 66
Chicken and Wild Rice Soup, 112
Chicken Fingers, 144
Chicken Pasta with Ham and
    Sun-Dried Tomatoes, 147

Chicken Potpie, 145
Chicken Saltimbocca with
    Country Ham, 143
Chicken Shish Kabobs, 146
Chicken Stir-Fry Lettuce Cups, 148
Chinese Chicken Wings, 46
Cilantro Lime Chicken Fajitas, 150
Cobb Salad Bites, 82
Cranberry Chicken, 142
Curry Chicken Salad, 81
Fresh Barbecued Chicken, 140
Fresh Chicken Soup, 110
Honey Cilantro Lime Chicken Salad, 81
Honey Walnut Chicken, 141
Indian Chicken, 142
Nutty Apricot Goat Cheese
    Chicken Salad, 83
Pasta with Chicken and
    Sun-Dried Tomatoes, 148
Pesto Chicken with Penne, 147
Santa Rosa Salad, 80
Spicy Coconut Soup, 111
Spicy White Chili, 109
Spinach Chicken Pasta Salad, 79
Sweet Potato Chicken Curry, 151
Thai Chicken in Spicy Peanut Sauce, 149
Tortilla Soup, 113
Wild Rice Casserole, 176
Yakitori, 144

Chili

Spicy White Chili, 109
Turkey and Vegetable Chili, 106
Turkey White Bean Chili, 107

Chocolate

Amano Artisan Chocolate
    Pots de Crème, 225
AvenueSweets Espresso Caramel
    Oat Bars, 218
Caramel Shortbread, 220
Chewy Brownie Cookies, 220
Chocolate Buttercream Frosting, 210
Chocolate Chip Bundt Cake, 210
Chocolate Frosting, 211

Chocolate Nut Meringues, 217
Chocolate Zucchini Bread, 27
Easy Brownies, 215
Fudge, 223
Graham Cracker Toffee Bark, 223
Oatmeal Chocolate Chip
    Coconut Cookies, 219
Orange Chocolate Chip Cookies, 222
Salted Fudge Brownies, 217
Upside-Down German Chocolate
    Cake, 212
Yogurt Chocolate Cake, 211

Cookies

Caramel Shortbread, 220
Chewy Brownie Cookies, 220
Chocolate Nut Meringues, 217
Favorite Oatmeal Cookies, 219
Molasses Spice Cookies, 221
Oatmeal Chocolate Chip
    Coconut Cookies, 219
Orange Chocolate Chip Cookies, 222
Pecan Spice Cookies, 221

Cookies, Bar

AvenueSweets Espresso Caramel
    Oat Bars, 218
Cheesecake Bars, 218
Easy Brownies, 215
Oatmeal Butterscotch Bars, 215
Salted Fudge Brownies, 217

Corn

Corn Cakes with Peach
    Mustard Sauce, 56
Corn, Cherry Tomato, Arugula and
    Blue Cheese Salad, 92
Fresh Corn Polenta with Sausage, Chard
    and Oyster Mushrooms, 136
Polenta, 136
Salmon Chowder, 115
Spicy White Chili, 109
Tamale Pie, 126
Turkey and Vegetable Chili, 106

Couscous
Couscous Salad, 85
Spinach Couscous Sauté, 173
Tapenade Lamb Kabobs and
Couscous, 156

Crab Meat
Crab Meat Spread, 65
Crab-Stuffed Pork Chops, 132
Log Haven Quinoa-Crusted
Crab Cakes, 158
Party Turnovers, 58

Cranberry
Cranberry Chicken, 142
Cranberry Jalapeño Salsa, 68
Curry Chicken Salad, 81
Holiday Cranberry Chutney with
Brie Cheese, 63
Orzo Wild Rice Salad, 86
Sweet and Nutty Quinoa, 173

Desserts. *See also* Cakes; Candies;
Cookies; Ice Cream; Pastries;
Pies; Sauces, Dessert; Tarts
Amano Artisan Chocolate
Pots de Crème, 225
Apple Crisp, 201
Apple Pie with Macadamia Nut
Crumble, 198
Caramel Banana Cake, 208
Carrot Cake, 209
Chocolate Chip Bundt Cake, 210
Cream Cheese Pound Cake, 213
Fresh Apricot Turnovers, 202
Fresh Peach Pie with Sunflower Seed
Crust, 200
Grilled Peaches, 202
Key Lime Pie, 199
Lehi Roller Mills Vanilla Cupcakes with
Raspberry Cream Cheese Frosting, 214
Peanut Butter Pie, 201
Raspberry Lemonade Sherbet, 205
Raspberry Pecan Torte, 207
Rhubarb Cake, 212

Strawberries with Slide Ridge
Honey Wine Vinegar, 203
Upside-Down German Chocolate
Cake, 212
Yogurt Chocolate Cake, 211

Dips
Blue Cheese Chicken Wing Dip, 66
Clam Dip, 66
Greek Layered Dip, 67
Green Goddess Dip, 67
Hell's Backbone Grill Goat
Cheese Fondue, 64
Yogurt Onion Dip, 68

Duck
Goldener Hirsch Inn's Duck Confit with
Riesling Choucroute, 157

Egg Dishes
Deviled Eggs with Tarragon and
Watercress, 50
Egg Casserole, 16
Jalapeño Goat Cheese Frittata, 15
Potato, Eggs and Chorizo Tacos, 18
Shirred Pancetta and Arugula Eggs, 16
Sunday Eggs, 17

Eggplant
Eggplant and Sausage Pasta, 137
Eggplant Parmesan Burger, 128

Fish. *See also* Salmon
Citrus Fish, 166
Fish Tacos, 165
Foil-Baked Halibut, 162
Tilapia in a Parmesan Cheese Sauce, 166

Frostings/Icings
Caramel Icing, 208
Chocolate Buttercream Frosting, 210
Chocolate Frosting, 211
Orange Cream Cheese Frosting, 209
Raspberry Cream Cheese Frosting, 214

Fruit. *See also* individual kinds
Arugula and Fig Salad with Blue Cheese
and Bacon Vinaigrette, 91
Fresh Apricot Turnovers, 202
Gorgonzola-Stuffed Dates, 51
Lime Rum Marinated Fruit, 35
Mango Salsa, 69
Rhubarb Cake, 212

Goat Cheese
Baked Goat Cheese, 61
Black Bean and Goat Cheese
Enchiladas, 167
Hell's Backbone Grill Goat
Cheese Fondue, 64
Jalapeño Goat Cheese Frittata, 15
Nutty Apricot Goat Cheese
Chicken Salad, 83
Quinoa Salad with Grilled Asparagus,
Goat Cheese and Black Olive
Vinaigrette, 88
Shrimp, Spinach and Goat Cheese
Pizza, 72

Goldener Hirsch Inn Restaurant
Goldener Hirsch Inn's Duck Confit with
Riesling Choucroute, 157

Grains. *See also* Couscous; Grits; Quinoa;
Rice; Side Dishes, Grains
Mushroom Barley, 176

Grits
Cheese Hominy Grits, 177
Salmon and Grits, 20

Ground Beef
Beef and Fresh Vegetable
Marinara Sauce, 125
Eggplant Parmesan Burger, 128
Papa Rellena, 127
Tamale Pie, 126

Ham
Antipasto Pasta Salad, 76

Chicken Pasta with Ham and
Sun-Dried Tomatoes, 147
Chicken Saltimbocca with
Country Ham, 143
Goldener Hirsch Inn's Duck Confit with
Riesling Choucroute, 157
Party Turnovers, 58
Pressed Italian Sandwich, 139
Ribollita, 104
Rustic Prosciutto and Provolone
Sandwich, 73
Sage and Prosciutto Popovers, 51
Shirred Pancetta and Arugula Eggs, 16

Hell's Backbone Grill
Hell's Backbone Grill Goat Cheese
Fondue, 64

Honey
Almond Honey Butter, 35
Bavarian Honey Butter, 35
Cinnamon Honey Butter, 35
Greek Yogurt, Honey and Poppy Seeds
with Blackberries, 33
Herb Salt-Rubbed Rack of Lamb with
Honey-Vinegar Reduction, 153
Honey Cilantro Lime Chicken Salad, 81
Honey Pecan Tart, 197
Honey Walnut Chicken, 141
Honey Walnuts, 141
Lemon Honey Butter, 35
Miller's Basic Honey Butter, 35
Orange Honey Butter, 35
Pago's Cinnamon Beets with Nut
Crunch and Truffle Honey, 75
Soy Honey Ginger Sauce, 44
Spiced Honey Butter, 35
Strawberries with Slide Ridge Honey
Wine Vinegar, 203
Vanilla Bean Ice Cream with Slide Ridge
Honey Wine Vinegar, 206

Ice Cream
Green Tea Ice Cream, 206
Lemon Custard Ice Cream, 205

Vanilla Bean Ice Cream with Slide Ridge
Honey Wine Vinegar, 206

Kale
Greens with Cannellini Beans and
Winter Squash, 182
Potato Kale Soup, 100
Ribollita, 104
Sautéed Kale or Collards, 183

Lamb
Greek Layered Dip, 67
Herb Salt-Rubbed Rack of Lamb with
Honey-Vinegar Reduction, 153
Marguerite Henderson's Coffee and
Spice Lamb Kabobs with Lemon
Mint Rice, 154
Spiced Morgan Valley Lamb Shoulder
Chops, 155
Tapenade Lamb Kabobs and
Couscous, 156
Utah's Own Promontory Cheddar
Lamb Burger, 73

Leeks
Bacon, Leek and Cheddar Cheese
Mini Quiches, 12
Leek and Potato Gratin, 184

Lehi Roller Mills
Lehi Roller Mills Vanilla Cupcakes with
Raspberry Cream Cheese Frosting, 214

Lemon/Lime
Cilantro Lime Chicken Fajitas, 150
Coconut Lime Risotto, 174
Cumin-Lime Dressing, 87
Key Lime Pie, 199
Lemon Aïoli Dipping Sauce, 49
Lemon Custard Ice Cream, 205
Lemon Honey Butter, 35
Lemon-Maple Vinaigrette, 97
Marguerite Henderson's Coffee and
Spice Lamb Kabobs with Lemon
Mint Rice, 154

Meditrina's Curry Lime Prawns, 159
Raspberry Lemonade Sherbet, 205
RealSalt Lemon Rice, 174
Shrimp with Lemon Herb
Butter Sauce, 160

Log Haven
Log Haven Quinoa-Crusted
Crab Cakes, 158

Market Street Grill
Market Street Sabayon Sauce, 213

Meditrina
Meditrina's Curry Lime Prawns, 159

Miller's Honey Company
Almond Honey Butter, 35
Bavarian Honey Butter, 35
Cinnamon Honey Butter, 35
Lemon Honey Butter, 35
Miller's Basic Honey Butter, 35
Orange Honey Butter, 35
Spiced Honey Butter, 35

Morgan Valley Lamb
Spiced Morgan Valley Lamb Shoulder
Chops, 155

Muffins
Apple Pecan Streusel Muffins, 30
Blueberry Crumble Muffins, 31

Mushrooms
Beef and Fresh Vegetable
Marinara Sauce, 125
Cheese-Stuffed Mushrooms, 50
Chicken Shish Kabobs, 146
Coconut Curry Cashew Quinoa, 172
Company Stroganoff, 121
Fresh Corn Polenta with Sausage, Chard
and Oyster Mushrooms, 136
Great Scott Salad, 95
Jalapeño Goat Cheese Frittata, 15
Lobster Quiche, 13

Mushroom Barley, 176
Party Turnovers, 58
Pork Ragù, 135
Pot Stickers, 45
Salmon and Grits, 20
Spicy Coconut Soup, 111
Stir-Fried Bok Choy and Shiitake
    Mushrooms, 168
Veal Marsala, 129

Naked Fish Japanese Bistro
Naked Fish Kudamono Salad, 96

Nuts. *See also* Almonds; Cashews;
    Pecans; Walnuts
Apple Pie with Macadamia Nut
    Crumble, 198
Hazelnut Zucchini Bread, 28
Sautéed Brussels Sprouts with
    Hazelnuts, 179
Sweet and Crunchy Salad, 98
Sweet-and-Spicy Nuts, 60
White Chocolate Tart with Honey-
    Roasted Peanut Crust, 196

Orange
Citrus Fish, 166
Citrus Salad Toss, 93
Fresh Fruit Salad, 34
Fresh Fruit with Orange Cream, 34
Marguerite Henderson's Grilled
    Herbed Shrimp, 49
Orange Chocolate Chip Cookies, 222
Orange Cream Cheese Frosting, 209
Orange Honey Butter, 35
Spinach Chicken Pasta Salad, 79

Pago
Pago's Cinnamon Beets with Nut
    Crunch and Truffle Honey, 75

Pasta
Antipasto Pasta Salad, 76
Asian Chicken Pasta Salad, 77
Basil Chicken Pasta Salad, 78

Chicken Pasta with Ham and
    Sun-Dried Tomatoes, 147
Company Stroganoff, 121
Eggplant and Sausage Pasta, 137
Garlic and Ginger Shrimp with
    Rice Noodles, 161
Orecchiette with Fresh
    Mozzarella Cheese, 169
Orzo Salad with Spinach and Feta, 86
Orzo Wild Rice Salad, 86
Pasta with Chicken and
    Sun-Dried Tomatoes, 148
Pesto Chicken with Penne, 147
Pork Ragù, 135
Shrimp with Lemon Herb
    Butter Sauce, 160
Spinach Chicken Pasta Salad, 79
Tiger Prawns with Tomatoes and
    Pasta, 160
Tortellini Soup with Sausage, 114

Pastry/Crust
All-Purpose Pie Crust, 198
Celery Seed Pastry, 145
Coconut Graham Cracker Crust, 199
Honey-Roasted Peanut Crust, 196
Sunflower Seed Pastry, 200
Tart Pastry, 197

Peach
Fresh Peach Pie with Sunflower Seed
    Crust, 200
Grilled Peaches, 202
Peach Mustard Sauce, 56
Peach Scones, 26

Peanut Butter
Peanut Butter Pie, 201
Thai Chicken in Spicy Peanut Sauce, 149

Peas
Couscous Salad, 85
Mongolian Beef with Bean Sprouts, 123
Spicy Coconut Soup, 111
Sweet Potato Chicken Curry, 151

Pecans
Apple Pecan Streusel Muffins, 30
Dried Cherry, Apple and Pecan Salad
    with Maple Dressing, 94
French Toast with Pecans, 21
Honey Pecan Tart, 197
Naked Fish Kudamono Salad, 96
Northwest Autumn Salad, 97
Pecan Spice Cookies, 221
Raspberry Pecan Torte, 207
Sugared Pecans, 93

Peppers
Baked Vegetables with Sour
    Cream, 192
Basil Chicken Pasta Salad, 78
Beef and Fresh Vegetable
    Marinara Sauce, 125
Chicken Shish Kabobs, 146
Chicken Stir-Fry Lettuce
    Cups, 148
Cilantro Lime Chicken Fajitas, 150
Egg Casserole, 16
Garlic and Ginger Shrimp with
    Rice Noodles, 161
Jalapeño Goat Cheese Frittata, 15
Pacific Salmon with Roasted Red
    Pepper Beurre Pomme, 164
Pressed Italian Sandwich, 139
Quinoa and Black Bean Salad, 87
Spinach Couscous Sauté, 173
Sweet and Crunchy Salad, 98
Tamale Pie, 126
Thai Chicken in Spicy Peanut
    Sauce, 149
Turkey and Vegetable Chili, 106

Pies/Pastries
Apple Pie with Macadamia Nut
    Crumble, 198
Fresh Apricot Turnovers, 202
Fresh Peach Pie with Sunflower Seed
    Crust, 200
Key Lime Pie, 199
Peanut Butter Pie, 201

Pork. *See also* Bacon; Ham; Sausage
    Apple-Stuffed Pork Chops, 131
    Asian Pork Tenderloin, 130
    Best Barbecued Spareribs, 134
    Crab-Stuffed Pork Chops, 132
    Mexican Pork, 134
    Porketta, 130
    Pork Ragù, 135
    Pot Stickers, 45
    Provençal Spareribs with Roasted
        Potatoes and Brussels Sprouts, 133

Potatoes
    Creamy au Gratin Potatoes, 185
    Dutch Oven Potatoes, 184
    Indian-Style Potatoes (Aloo Subji), 187
    Leek and Potato Gratin, 184
    Papa Rellena, 127
    Potato, Eggs and Chorizo Tacos, 18
    Potato Gratin with Smoked Gouda, 186
    Potato Kale Soup, 100
    Potato Salad, 90
    Potato Soufflé, 186
    Provençal Spareribs with Roasted
        Potatoes and Brussels Sprouts, 133
    Ribollita, 104
    Roasted Garlic Beef Stew, 124
    Roasted Jalapeño, Bacon and
        Potato Soup, 99
    Salmon Chowder, 115
    Vegetarian Tikka Masala, 169

Pumpkin
    Curry Pumpkin Soup, 101

Quiche
    Bacon, Leek and Cheddar Cheese
        Mini Quiches, 12
    Lobster Quiche, 13
    Vegetable Quiche, 13

Quinoa
    Coconut Curry Cashew Quinoa, 172
    Log Haven Quinoa-Crusted
        Crab Cakes, 158

    Quinoa and Black Bean Salad, 87
    Quinoa Salad with Grilled Asparagus,
        Goat Cheese and Black Olive
        Vinaigrette, 88
    Sweet and Nutty Quinoa, 173

Raspberry
    Fresh Fruit Salad, 34
    Lehi Roller Mills Vanilla Cupcakes with
        Raspberry Cream Cheese Frosting, 214
    Nutty Apricot Goat Cheese
        Chicken Salad, 83
    Raspberry Compote, 23
    Raspberry Freezer Jam, 214
    Raspberry Lemonade Sherbet, 205
    Raspberry Pancakes, 23
    Raspberry Pecan Torte, 207
    Raspberry Sauce, 207

RealSalt
    RealSalt Chips, 69
    RealSalt Lemon Rice, 174

Rice
    Baked Stuffed Flank Steak, 118
    Chicken and Wild Rice Soup, 112
    Coconut Lime Risotto, 174
    Lemon Mint Rice, 154
    Mexican Rice with Cilantro Dressing, 175
    Orzo Wild Rice Salad, 86
    RealSalt Lemon Rice, 174
    Santa Rosa Salad, 80
    Wild Rice Casserole, 176

Salad Dressings
    Apricot Salad Dressing, 83
    Asian Salad Dressing, 77
    Bacon Vinaigrette, 91
    Black Olive Vinaigrette, 88
    Blue Cheese Salad Dressing, 82
    Citrus Salad Dressing, 93
    Cumin-Lime Dressing, 87
    Dijon Mustard Salad Dressing, 80
    Italian Salad Dressing, 78
    Kudamono Salad Dressing, 96

    Lemon-Maple Vinaigrette, 97
    Maple Dressing, 94
    Mustard Vinaigrette, 95
    Red Wine Vinaigrette, 98
    Sesame Seed Salad Dressing, 79

Salads
    Antipasto Pasta Salad, 76
    Arugula and Fig Salad with Blue Cheese
        and Bacon Vinaigrette, 91
    Asian Chicken Pasta Salad, 77
    Basil Chicken Pasta Salad, 78
    Citrus Salad Toss, 93
    Cobb Salad Bites, 82
    Corn, Cherry Tomato, Arugula and
        Blue Cheese Salad, 92
    Couscous Salad, 85
    Cucumber Salad, 90
    Curry Chicken Salad, 81
    Dried Cherry, Apple and Pecan Salad
        with Maple Dressing, 94
    Frisée Salad, 158
    Great Scott Salad, 95
    Honey Cilantro Lime Chicken Salad, 81
    Naked Fish Kudamono Salad, 96
    Northwest Autumn Salad, 97
    Nutty Apricot Goat Cheese
        Chicken Salad, 83
    Orzo Salad with Spinach and Feta, 86
    Orzo Wild Rice Salad, 86
    Panzanella, 89
    Potato Salad, 90
    Quinoa and Black Bean Salad, 87
    Quinoa Salad with Grilled Asparagus,
        Goat Cheese and Black Olive
        Vinaigrette, 88
    Santa Rosa Salad, 80
    Spinach Chicken Pasta Salad, 79
    Sweet and Crunchy Salad, 98

Salmon
    Cedar-Planked Salmon with
        Chef's Dressing, 163
    Pacific Salmon with Roasted Red
        Pepper Beurre Pomme, 164

Salmon and Grits, 20
Salmon Chowder, 115
Squatters' Captain Bastard's Stout
    Salmon, 162

Salsas
Cranberry Jalapeño Salsa, 68
Mango Salsa, 69
Tomatillo Salsa, 167

Sandwiches
Eggplant Parmesan Burger, 128
Pressed Italian Sandwich, 139
Rustic Prosciutto and Provolone
    Sandwich, 73
Utah's Own Promontory Cheddar
    Lamb Burger, 73

Sauces, Dessert
Market Street Sabayon Sauce, 213
Raspberry Sauce, 207

Sauces, Savory
Balsamic Marinade, 181
Barbecue Sauce, 119, 140
Cilantro Dressing, 175
Cilantro Yogurt Sauce, 142
Ginger Marinade, 181
Honey-Vinegar Reduction, 153
Lemon Aïoli Dipping Sauce, 49
Peach Mustard Sauce, 56
Peanut Dipping Sauce, 47
Soy Honey Ginger Sauce, 44

Sausage
Egg Casserole, 16
Eggplant and Sausage Pasta, 137
Fresh Corn Polenta with
    Sausage, Chard and Oyster
    Mushrooms, 136
Potato, Eggs and Chorizo Tacos, 18
Sausage Stuffing, 177
Tortellini Soup with Sausage, 114
Wild Rice Casserole, 176
Zucchini Sausage Squares, 19

Seafood. *See also* Crab Meat;
    Fish; Shrimp
Clam Dip, 66
Lobster Quiche, 13

Shrimp
Couscous Salad, 85
Garlic and Ginger Shrimp with
    Rice Noodles, 161
Log Haven Quinoa-Crusted
    Crab Cakes, 158
Marguerite Henderson's Grilled
    Herbed Shrimp, 49
Meditrina's Curry Lime
    Prawns, 159
Sassy Shrimp, 46
Shrimp, Spinach and Goat Cheese
    Pizza, 72
Shrimp with Lemon Herb
    Butter Sauce, 160
Skewered Shrimp with
    Peanut Dipping Sauce, 47
Tiger Prawns with Tomatoes and
    Pasta, 160

Side Dishes, Grains
Cheese Hominy Grits, 177
Coconut Curry Cashew
    Quinoa, 172
Coconut Lime Risotto, 174
Lemon Mint Rice, 154
Mexican Rice with Cilantro
    Dressing, 175
Mushroom Barley, 176
RealSalt Lemon Rice, 174
Sausage Stuffing, 177
Spinach Couscous Sauté, 173
Sweet and Nutty Quinoa, 173
Wild Rice Casserole, 176

Side Dishes, Vegetables
Baked Basil Tomatoes, 191
Baked Vegetables with Sour Cream, 192
Barbecued Beans, 180
Broccolini, 180

Butternut Squash Gratin, 189
Creamy au Gratin Potatoes, 185
Dutch Oven Potatoes, 184
Festive Holiday Green Beans, 179
Greens with Cannellini Beans and
    Winter Squash, 182
Indian-Style Potatoes (Aloo Subji), 187
Leek and Potato Gratin, 184
Marinated Beets, 181
Potato Gratin with Smoked Gouda, 186
Potato Soufflé, 186
Roasted Carrots and Shallots, 183
Roasted Cherry Tomatoes, 192
Sautéed Brussels Sprouts with
    Hazelnuts, 179
Sautéed Kale or Collards, 183
Sweet Potato Casserole, 190
Zucchini Fans, 191

Slide Ridge Honey
Strawberries with Slide Ridge Honey
    Wine Vinegar, 203
Vanilla Bean Ice Cream with Slide Ridge
    Honey Wine Vinegar, 206

Snacks
Black Pepper Almonds, 59
Black Pepper Crackers, 64
Camembert Cheese Crisps, 60
RealSalt Chips, 69
Sweet-and-Spicy Nuts, 60
White Pepper Cashews, 59

Soups. *See also* Chili
Chicken and Wild Rice Soup, 112
Curry Pumpkin Soup, 101
Fresh Chicken Soup, 110
Grilled Tomato Soup, 105
Moroccan Carrot and
    Sweet Potato Soup, 103
Potato Kale Soup, 100
Ribollita, 104
Roasted Jalapeño, Bacon and
    Potato Soup, 99
Salmon Chowder, 115

Spicy Coconut Soup, 111
Tortellini Soup with Sausage, 114
Tortilla Soup, 113
Zucchini Soup, 101

Spinach
Asian Chicken Pasta Salad, 77
Orzo Salad with Spinach and Feta, 86
Shrimp, Spinach and Goat Cheese
Pizza, 72
Spinach Chicken Pasta Salad, 79
Spinach Couscous Sauté, 173

Spreads
Amaretto and Brie Cheese, 61
Baked Goat Cheese, 61
Crab Meat Spread, 65
Holiday Cranberry Chutney with
Brie Cheese, 63
Utah's Own Arugula Pesto, 57
White Bean Hummus, 65

Squash
Baked Vegetables with Sour Cream, 192
Butternut Squash Gratin, 189
Frisée Salad, 158
Greens with Cannellini Beans and
Winter Squash, 182
Vegetarian Tikka Masala, 169

Squatters Pub Brewery
Squatters' Captain Bastard's Stout
Salmon, 162

Strawberry
Citrus Salad Toss, 93
Fresh Fruit Salad, 34

Fresh Fruit with Orange Cream, 34
Naked Fish Kudamono Salad, 96
Strawberries with Slide Ridge
Honey Wine Vinegar, 203

Sweet Potatoes
Moroccan Carrot and
Sweet Potato Soup, 103
Sweet Potato Casserole, 190
Sweet Potato Chicken Curry, 151

Tarts
Honey Pecan Tart, 197
White Chocolate Tart with
Honey-Roasted Peanut Crust, 196

Tea Grotto, The
Polenta Pesto Squares, 57
Utah's Own Arugula Pesto, 57

Tomatoes
Antipasto Pasta Salad, 76
Baked Basil Tomatoes, 191
Chicken Pasta with Ham and
Sun-Dried Tomatoes, 147
Corn, Cherry Tomato, Arugula and
Blue Cheese Salad, 92
Grilled Tomato Soup, 105
Orecchiette with Fresh
Mozzarella Cheese, 169
Pasta with Chicken and Sun-Dried
Tomatoes, 148
Roasted Cherry Tomatoes, 192
Tiger Prawns with Tomatoes and
Pasta, 160
Tortilla Soup, 113
Turkey and Vegetable Chili, 106

Turkey
Asian Meatballs with Soy Honey
Ginger Sauce, 44
Turkey and Vegetable Chili, 106
Turkey Vegetable Meat Loaf, 151
Turkey White Bean Chili, 107

Veal
Veal Marsala, 129

Vegetables. See also individual kinds
Chicken Potpie, 145
Cucumber Salad, 90
Panzanella, 89

Walnuts
Chocolate Nut Meringues, 217
Honey Walnuts, 141
Nutty Apricot Goat Cheese
Chicken Salad, 83
Nutty Honey Granola, 33
Oatmeal Butterscotch Bars, 215
Walnut Shortcake Biscuits, 26

Zucchini
Chicken Pasta with Ham and
Sun-Dried Tomatoes, 147
Chicken Shish Kabobs, 146
Chocolate Zucchini Bread, 27
Hazelnut Zucchini Bread, 28
Jalapeño Goat Cheese Frittata, 15
Turkey and Vegetable Chili, 106
Turkey Vegetable Meat Loaf, 151
Zucchini Fans, 191
Zucchini Sausage Squares, 19
Zucchini Soup, 101

SALT TO HONEY
RECIPES FOR GREAT GATHERINGS